Cambridge El

Elements in Contentious Politics
edited by
David S. Meyer
University of California, Irvine
Suzanne Staggenborg
University of Pittsburgh

MOBILIZING FOR ABORTION RIGHTS IN LATIN AMERICA

Mariela Daby
Reed College

Mason W. Moseley
West Virginia University

CAMBRIDGE
UNIVERSITY PRESS

Shaftesbury Road, Cambridge CB2 8EA, United Kingdom

One Liberty Plaza, 20th Floor, New York, NY 10006, USA

477 Williamstown Road, Port Melbourne, VIC 3207, Australia

314–321, 3rd Floor, Plot 3, Splendor Forum, Jasola District Centre,
New Delhi – 110025, India

103 Penang Road, #05–06/07, Visioncrest Commercial, Singapore 238467

Cambridge University Press is part of Cambridge University Press & Assessment,
a department of the University of Cambridge.

We share the University's mission to contribute to society through the pursuit of
education, learning and research at the highest international levels of excellence.

www.cambridge.org
Information on this title: www.cambridge.org/9781009452748

DOI: 10.1017/9781009452724

First published 2023

A catalogue record for this publication is available from the British Library

ISBN 978-1-009-45274-8 Hardback
ISBN 978-1-009-45271-7 Paperback
ISSN 2633-3570 (online)
ISSN 2633-3562 (print)

Mobilizing for Abortion Rights in Latin America

Elements in Contentious Politics

DOI: 10.1017/9781009452724
First published online: December 2023

Mariela Daby
Reed College

Mason W. Moseley
West Virginia University

Author for correspondence: Mariela Daby, mariela@reed.edu

Abstract: The past decade has seen sweeping changes in terms of reproductive rights in Latin America. Argentina and Uruguay have fully legalized abortion in the first twelve weeks of pregnancy. Some countries, like Chile, have loosened restrictions; others like El Salvador, Honduras, and the Dominican Republic have maintained or even tightened some of the most punitive abortion laws in the world. Abortion rights even vary within countries – in Mexico, the practice has been fully legal in certain states, and punishable with jail time in others. This Element explains how feminist social movements have transformed the politics of abortion in Latin America.

Keywords: abortion, social movements, gender, Latin America, protest

ISBNs: 9781009452748 (HB), 9781009452717 (PB), 9781009452724 (OC)
ISSNs: 2633-3570 (online), 2633-3562 (print)

Contents

1 The Battle Over Abortion Rights in Latin America

Early on the morning of December 30, 2020, thousands of Argentine women gathered in front of the National Congress building in Buenos Aires, anxiously awaiting the results of a Senate vote that was years in the making. After rejecting a similar bill in 2018, the Senate was debating another bill that would legalize abortion during the first fourteen weeks of pregnancy. If the bill passed, Argentina would become the largest Latin American country to legalize abortion in the most Catholic region in the world. Around 1:00 a.m., a big screen facing the multitude of women clad in green handkerchiefs revealed the final vote tally. Abortion was law in Argentina. Tens of thousands of women in the plaza, and in plazas like it across the country, rejoiced.

The groundswell of women in the Plaza del Congreso was nothing new, Beginning with the mass mobilization that occurred following the murder of Chiara Páez in 2015 – which birthed a social movement against gender violence that would become known as Ni Una Menos ("Not One [Woman] Less"; NUM). Páez was fourteen years old and three months pregnant when her boyfriend killed and buried her in his grandparents' backyard. The NUM movement spread across the region making feminist mobilization a way of life in Argentina. Within a year of its emergence, NUM had adopted abortion rights as a part of its set of claims, and an abortion rights campaign was born. "Without legal abortion, there is no 'ni una menos,'" read the manifesto on the NUM website. By 2017, the long-taboo subject of women's reproductive rights had made its way into the mainstream, a topic of debate at high schools and universities, cafes, and on nightly talk shows that reached millions of Argentines at their dinner tables.

What is puzzling about the push for abortion rights in Argentina is that few could have predicted it, given common explanations of abortion rights expansion. Research indicates that countries will experience changes in abortion policy when they are governed by a leftist party or governing coalition (Blofield and Ewig 2017), when the issue is supported by a majority of citizens (i.e., there are widespread shifts in public opinion) and when the society becomes more secular over the course of time (Wood et al. 2016). The growing mobilization by feminist activists and initial 2018 bill that passed in the Chamber of Deputies before failing in the Senate occurred during the government of conservative President Mauricio Macri, who opposed legalization. Furthermore, there was no obvious shift in terms of public opinion regarding abortion in the years leading up to the debate, and Argentines actually reported higher levels of religiosity in 2017 than a decade prior (AmericasBarometer 2017).

What *had* changed was the presence of tens of thousands of Argentine women in the streets, initially to protest against gender violence, and then to claim control over their own bodies in the face of mounting hospitalizations and deaths as a result of unsafe, clandestine abortions.

Sidney Tarrow defines social movements as "collective challenges, based on common purposes and social solidarities, in sustained interaction with elites, opponents, and authorities" (1994: 4). In Argentina, a budding abortion rights social movement framed the issue as inseparable from economic inequality. Prohibition had not stopped women from seeking abortions – rather it forced poor women without the resources to seek out reputable health care providers to abort in unsafe conditions. Instead of grounding their claims in philosophical or theological arguments about the origins of life and the viability of the fetus or the right to privacy, activists framed abortion as a question of social justice and public health. "The rich abort, the poor die," said the posters at rallies. In the most unequal region of the world, the proabortion movement tapped into a resonant vein of social movement discourse.

The Argentine experience buoyed the spirits of reproductive rights advocates across the region, who doubled down on their efforts to reform abortion laws in their countries. Similar to NUM, which spread like wildfire in Latin America, proabortion activists in Brazil, Chile, and Mexico co-opted the green "pañuelo" (handkerchief) made famous by the Argentine movement. In Colombia and Mexico, abortion rights movements won massive victories in the Supreme Court, following different paths to decriminalization than the legislative avenue that worked in Argentina and Uruguay. At the same time, other Latin American countries experienced a backlash. In countries like El Salvador and Nicaragua, conservative parties collaborated with the Catholic Church and a growing Evangelical movement to pressure governments to maintain restrictions on abortion access, and even make the laws on the books *more* punitive.

Why did Argentina legalize abortion when it did? And what explains the diverging trajectories in terms of reproductive rights that we observe across the region? This Element in the *Cambridge Elements Series in Contentious Politics* examines the crucial role that social movements and mass mobilization play in the fight over abortion rights in Latin America.

1.1 Shifting Tides in Reproductive Rights

The past decade has seen sweeping changes in terms of reproductive rights in Latin America – a region once thought to be the unlikeliest of places for such a social transformation to occur. Latin America is the heart of modern Catholicism, and throughout the twentieth century lagged behind European and North American democracies on social issues like divorce and reproductive justice. The taboo nature of abortion and contraception made reform unlikely,

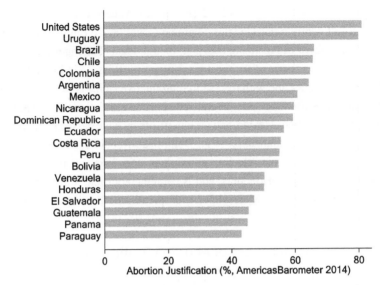

Figure 1 Abortion is justified when the mother's health is at risk (AmericasBarometer 2014).

even as millions of clandestine abortions continued to occur, many of which were performed in dangerous conditions (Kulczycki 2011).

As Latin American democracies consolidated in the 1990s, legislatures have revisited abortion laws and, in some cases, loosened restrictions to allow abortion in cases of rape or risk to the mother's life (Blofield and Ewig 2017). From 1999 to 2016, eight Latin American countries in total revised abortion laws, though elective abortion was mostly off the table. Yet it was apparent that abortion had lost its taboo status, and further changes might be on the horizon. As Kulczycki noted in 2011, "Conflict over how abortion should be managed, and particularly over its legal availability, is likely to be more difficult to contain as societies become more open and women gain greater choices and more influence. Awareness of the public health risks stemming from restrictive laws continues to grow" (2011: 215). By 2014, majorities believed that abortion was justified when the mother's health was at risk in most Latin American countries, according to survey data from the Latin American Public Opinion Project (Figure 1).[1]

Uruguay, spurred by widespread feminist mobilization and a strong left party in the Frente Amplio (Broad Front), became the first Latin American democracy

---

[1] This measure of abortion support is drawn from an item included in the AmericasBarometer surveys, which asks individuals whether abortion is justified when the mother's health is at risk (0 = "no," 1 = "yes, it is justified"). We follow prior work on the topic in labeling this variable "abortion justification" (Cohen and Evans 2018).

to legalize elective abortion in 2012 (Fernández Anderson 2017). Argentina followed suit nearly a decade later. Supreme Courts in Colombia and Mexico have ruled in favor of legalizing abortion, though legal challenges loom on the horizon. Abortion is one of the most pressing political issues in Latin America today, and the landscape with respect to reproductive rights is in constant flux; while numerous countries have liberalized abortion restrictions in recent years (e.g., Argentina, Chile, Mexico, and Uruguay), others have passed punitive laws that entrench its criminalization (e.g., Dominican Republic, El Salvador, and Nicaragua). In Colombia, elective abortion is now legal up to twenty-four weeks. In El Salvador, Honduras, and Nicaragua, abortion is even banned in cases of rape and incest. Meanwhile, widespread mobilization on both sides continues unabated.

1.2 Existing Explanations of Abortion Politics in Latin America

Studies of reproductive rights have highlighted the decline of organized religion, shifts in public opinion, the strength of progressive political parties, feminist mobilization, and other institutional factors as necessary conditions for abortion legalization. Without an increasingly secular society, supportive public opinion, leftist governments, strong feminist movements, progressive courts, activists, politicians, and public health officials, liberalization of abortion laws would seem unlikely.[2]

1.2.1 Secularization

A decline in religiosity – measured below as the importance of religion in people's lives – has been theorized to presage the push for abortion legalization. In Latin America, the power of institutionalized Christianity is the most significant antiabortion force. The Church defends the right to life from conception and envisions abortion as murder. Activists and politicians who seek to legalize abortion are "fighting organized Christianity" (Corrales 2021: 2).[3] And whereas some countries in the region observed an increase in the number of people who do not identify with any religion (Somma et al. 2017), and the rise of "Light Catholicism" (Corrales 2021: 22), tolerance and acceptance for abortion have not significantly changed. The Church has publicly threatened to excommunicate those who support abortion legalization, a considerable threat in a region

---

[2] Abortion is legalized when it is not considered a crime. Abortion is decriminalized when it is not subject to prosecution under any circumstances during a period of time (usually during the first trimester). Liberalization should just imply that the conditions under which women can get abortions are expanded.

[3] The original quote references both reproductive and LGBTQ rights.

where the majority, 83.7 percent of politicians, identify as Catholics (Alcántara and Rivas 2018; Fernández Anderson 2021).

Beyond the influential Catholic Church, the popular and ever-growing Evangelical movement in Latin America holds conservative views about reproductive and LGBTQ rights (Boas 2020; Corrales 2021). Hence, even when we observe changes in the way citizens identify religiously, the new alliance between Evangelicals and Catholics suggests that religion is a key variable in understanding abortion criminalization.

Explaining abortion decriminalization requires that we examine how and when political actors can confront and win a fight against one of the world's oldest and most powerful institutions. For a long time, reproductive rights, and especially abortion, were not even publicly discussed as they were envisioned as issues that wasted votes ("pianta votos") while antagonizing the powerful Catholic Church (Fernández Anderson 2021). Is it the decline of organized religion, or religiosity more broadly, that explains why abortion has suddenly become a wedge issue in Latin American politics?

While proabortion movements across the region have certainly challenged the cultural hegemony of the Catholic Church, there is some evidence that religiosity has actually *increased* across the region in recent years (Smith 2018; Daby and Moseley 2022). In 2013, Pope Francis became the head of the Catholic Church. As the first pope from the Americas born in Buenos Aires, Francis has a more tolerant and welcoming position for members of the LGBT community, but sustains traditional views of the Church about abortion. In Argentina, for example, 71 percent of citizens continue to identify as Catholic and over 90 percent have favorable views of the pope (Pew Research Center's Religion & Public Life Project 2014). Moreover, it is unclear why a decline in the importance of religion would drive decriminalization in some contexts, and retrenchment in others.

Figure 2 presents results from an estimated ordinary least squares (OLS) regression model of abortion justification, drawing on survey data from fifteen countries in Latin America (AmericasBarometer 2014). The results illustrate the extent to which other individual-level variables correlate with abortion support. In these individual-level models of abortion justification, religiosity has a significant negative effect – in other words, the more religious one is, the less likely they are to support abortion rights. Another piece of evidence that also seems consistent with the secularization argument is that educational attainment is the strongest individual-level determinant of support for abortion rights, as highly educated individuals tend to be less religious (Casanova 2007; Figure 3). But these results tell us little about the distribution of religious and educated individuals, nor the motivations of politicians who have shifted course

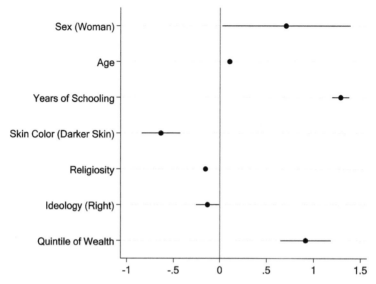

Figure 2 Individual-level correlates of abortion justification
(AmericasBarometer 2014)[4]

on reproductive rights. A decline in the importance of religion alone thus seems insufficient to explain the current inflexion point in Latin American's relationship with abortion.

1.2.2 Public Opinion

Changes in public opinion are often used to explain significant changes in moral policy.[5] The idea is that changes in public policy become possible when a sizable portion of the population changes their views on moral policy issues (see Page and Shapiro 1983; Loftus 2001; Wood et al. 2016). Causality, nevertheless, should be addressed in studying changes in public opinion and policy. For example, in her study of abortion decriminalization in Spain, Blofield (2006) shows that changes in public opinion took place *after* policy changes.

Our work takes public opinion seriously because we know that politicians take polls into account in making political decisions, and in Latin America's democratic era, voters shape public policy through elections. Furthermore, in regimes in Latin America where protests are frequent (Moseley 2018), the

---

[4] Results of an OLS regression model of abortion justification (0 = "no"; 1 = "yes"). Question wording is available at lapopsurverys.org and variable coding follows Moseley (2018). Replication materials can be found at marieladaby.com.

[5] Moral policy refers to political regulations about social values such as sexual and reproductive rights. Same-sex marriage and abortion are examples of moral policy (Díez 2015).

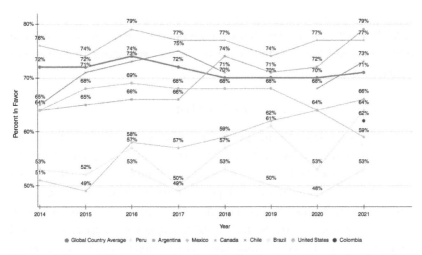

Figure 3 Favorability toward abortion legalization over time in the Americas

temperature on the streets is used to push for policy change. Illustrative of this argument is the public change of opinion of former president of Argentina, Cristina Fernández de Kirchner, who explicitly stated that she changed her opinion about abortion legalization from being against its legalization to supporting it due to the presence of the women and girls in the streets during the debate in the Congress.

Figure 3 highlights to extent to which attitudes regarding abortion have shifted in Latin America over the past decade. According to public opinion data from Ipsos, while the global average in terms of abortion favorability has remained somewhat constant, a number of Latin American countries have experienced significant boosts in support.[6] Among the biggest movers is Mexico, where abortion support increased from about 50 percent in 2014 to 66 percent in 2021. Brazil has undergone a similar sea change, and in Argentina, abortion rights now count on higher levels of popular support than in Canada or the United States.

But did changes in public opinion regarding abortion rights cause the debate to emerge, or vice versa? A closer look at the timing of opinion shifts reveals that significant turns in public opinion seem to have occurred *following* mass mobilization in the streets, and the introduction of abortion rights on the policy agenda. Prior to 2017, positive attitudes toward abortion experienced only an incremental uptick. In Argentina, the most significant positive shift in abortion justification occurred after a decriminalization bill was introduced in

---

[6] For Ipsos, this measure counts individuals who approve of abortion whenever a woman wants one or under certain conditions: www.ipsos.com/en/global-views-abortion-2021.

Congress in 2018 (Daby and Moseley 2022). While Latin Americans have certainly moderated in their views on reproductive rights, it is unclear that public opinion drove the abortion debate, or if it was actually the other way around.

1.2.3 The Left

The left, broadly defined as progressive incumbents or a strong coalition of left parties in government, has been associated with changes in reproductive rights given its historical commitment toward equality (Friedman 2009; Blofield and Ewig 2017). In Latin America, the type of left party is essential to understand abortion decriminalization. Institutionalized left parties are more likely to liberalize reproductive rights than populist left governments (Blofield and Ewig 2017: 481). In recent years, abortion has found its way on the policy agenda in countries with conservative presidents (Argentina), and even been fully decriminalized in countries where rightist parties govern (Colombia). Clearly, the odds of passing legislation that liberalizes abortion law increase exponentially when programmatic left parties are in power. But the legislative process is not the only pathway that abortion rights movements have leveraged to pursue their goals.

1.2.4 Class

In Latin America, the most unequal region in the world, class differences imply that abortions are safe and accessible to nonpoor women, but often result in injury or death for poor women who abort in unsafe conditions (Kulczycki 2011). As a result, building a women's movement to legalize abortion is more challenging than in cases where all women, regardless of class, are unable to access safe abortions (Htun and Weldon 2018).[7] This difference contributes to explain why divorce and same-sex marriage, two moral policies that were also strongly opposed by the Catholic Church, were passed much earlier than abortion. Being unable to get a divorce or marry affects all individuals regardless of their class status.

What was once believed a barrier to liberalization became a key component of social movement strategy. Throughout the region, abortion rights activists have appealed to conceptions of social justice to advocate for removing restrictions on abortion access. Class cleavages overlap with racial inequality in Latin

---

[7] Htun and Weldon (2018) argue that legalized abortion is a doctrinal and status issue. Legalization goes against the established doctrine of organized Catholicism and is a policy that empowers women as a status group. This is because women of different classes have different access to safe underground abortion based on their income.

America, but class-based movements have historically provided the foundation for social and economic progress throughout the region. By educating fellow citizens about the disproportionate burden carried by poor women with respect to abortion bans, abortion rights movements have weaponized inequality and turned a weakness into a strength. Latin American citizens understand the language of social and economic justice, and linking abortion rights to this storied history has become an effective strategy in the fight for abortion rights.

1.2.5 Issue Networks

Some argue that state and nonstate actors, together with activists and professionals, work together to achieve abortion legalization. The controversy in the literature is about the relationship and causality of social movements and activists. Instead of using social movements to refer to nonstate actors, scholars interested in explaining public policy change refer to policy networks (Kubal 2012), issue networks (Htun 2003), and networks (Hochstetler and Keck 2007; Díez 2015). Some scholars argue that activists are the ones who form these networks (Díez 2015), while others (Htun 2003) state that these networks emerge as a result of common interests in a particular policy area, in this case, abortion. The argument is that these networks influence state and nonstate actors' policy choices and contribute to shaping a supportive climate in public opinion.

1.2.6 Descriptive Representation

Countries in the region have been implementing different versions of gender quotas, including parity laws, since the 1990s. A recent overview of the literature shows that quotas are followed by greater legislative attention to "issues related to women's rights, public health, and poverty alleviation" (Clayton 2021: 235). The two ways quotas affect public policy are by broadly changing legislators' behavior by altering the composition of the legislature, and shifting preferences by organizing collectively to affect legislative decisions, seem to explain changes in abortion policy in some Latin American countries. Building on a substantive body of research, Clayton shows that "women legislators participate more actively and more emotively in debates on women's rights and other gendered issue areas than do men" (241).[8]

In Latin America, the implementation of gender quotas led to an increase in the number of women in Congress changing the environment – from

---

[8] See also Catalano (2019), Clayton et al. (2017), Dietrich, Bryce J., Matthew Hayes, and Diana Z. O'Brien. 2019. "Pitch Perfect: Vocal Pitch and the Emotional Intensity of Congressional Speech." *American Political Science Review* 113 (4): 941–62. https://doi.org/10.1017/S0003055419000467. Osborn and Mendez (2010), Pearson and Dancey (2011), and Piscopo (2011).

a majoritarian male legislature to a more mixed gender environment – and the discussions in Congress. Paraphrasing feminist scholar Mariana Caminotti (2013) quotas helped to "feminize" the political agenda ("feminizar la agenda política"). Research shows that quotas enable women legislators to sponsor bills related to women's rights on issues of reproduction and violence against women (Schwindt-Bayer 2006; Franceschet and Piscopo 2008). By enlarging the number of women in Congress and incorporating women's rights in the political agenda, quotas contributed to the discussion of abortion legalization.

Women legislators who had benefited from quotas played a central role in advancing reproductive rights in many Latin American countries. In the case of Argentina, the construction of a legislative block of women from different political parties identified as "the sisterhood" ("las sororas") was central in giving the bill visibility and support. Silvia Lospenato, a deputy from the right-wing president's political party (Propuesta Republicana [PRO]) gave one of the most powerful, emotional, and memorable speeches of the long session that captured the sense of time, change, and emotions that had been on displayed on the streets surrounding the Congress.[9] In her discourse, Silvia Lospenato mentioned and recognized all the actors who had participated in the fight to expand the rights for girls and women: "I came to politics for that reason: to address real problems. For the sisterhood, the multi-partisan group of women who came to Argentine politics to stay ... united in our differences, always supporting women. For the women in our homes, our mothers and daughters ... we want abortion to be legal, safe, and free. That it be law."

Beyond gender quotas, the region has had female politicians elected to the highest office, the Presidency. Since the return of democracy in the region, Argentina, Brazil, Chile, Panama, and Costa Rica had elected female presidents with different personal viewpoints about abortion. We examine some of these cases in detail and highlight how gender and politics play a role in female presidents' decision to support or oppose bills about abortion legalization. However, almost every country in Latin America has gender quotas, but not all Latin American countries have legalized abortion. Indeed, none of the perspectives listed above fully explain why abortion has become such a critical wedge issue in Latin American politics in recent years, and more importantly, why countries have diverged in terms of reproductive rights access.

---

[9]   The session lasted twenty-three hours and it was described as "strenuous, historic, and dramatic." Silvina Lospenato explaining how she changed her discourse in the midst of hearing the women on the streets, said, "At dawn, when it seemed that we were going to lose the vote and hearing that crowd of women in the streets, I thought that if the law was not going to pass, we at least needed a speech that said that we were going to keep fighting for that right" (quoted in Roffo 2020).

1.3 Mobilizing for Abortion Rights in Latin America

We argue that mass mobilization has transformed the politics of abortion in Latin America today. In many countries, feminist social movements have changed the political agenda, as street activism in favor of loosening restrictions on abortion access has swelled in recent years. Governments have created state bureaucracies, even ministries dedicated to gender issues, and mass media has evolved to reflect cultural shifts fueled by feminist mobilization. Family relations among grandparents, parents, and daughters are also changing. Abortion, although still illegal in many countries, has begun to lose its taboo status. Yet this shift in norms in the most Catholic region in the world has produced a backlash in many countries, fueling a push for more punitive laws from movements on the right.

Our argument begins with the assumption that increasingly, key political debates in Latin America start in the streets (Moseley 2015, 2018). While one might reasonably argue that democracy is "the only game in town" in many Latin American countries (Przeworski 1991), institutions remain weak in many regimes, meaning that they are characterized by low levels of enforcement and high levels of temporal instability (Brinks et al. 2019). Bountiful evidence suggests that where institutions are weak, contention thrives, as citizens lacking faith in formal representational channels adopt contentious behaviors to make claims (Machado et al. 2011; Boulding 2014; Moseley 2018). Rates of protest have increased in the region in the democratic era, and many key policy debates play out in the streets.

The movement for abortion rights in Latin America has been around for decades, but long struggled to build support and gain powerful allies in politics, given the taboo surrounding the issue and the strength of the Catholic Church. But as rates of protest have increased in recent years, social movements have succeeded in placing issues on the agenda that had long been impolitic on the left. Caving to pressure from civic organizations, Chile became the last Latin American country to legalize divorce in 2004. In 2010, Argentina became the first Latin American country to legalize same-sex marriage, and soon Brazil (2013), Uruguay (2013), Colombia (2016), and others followed (Díez 2015). In 2012, Argentina was again the pioneer when it allowed transgender individuals to change their legal name and official identity based on their gender identity, and in 2021 the country added a third gender option on all national ID cards.

Abortion rights mobilization has been on the rise in Latin America since 2015 (Figure 4). We collected data on protest events surrounding the issue – including proabortion and antiabortion rallies – in the two newspapers with widest

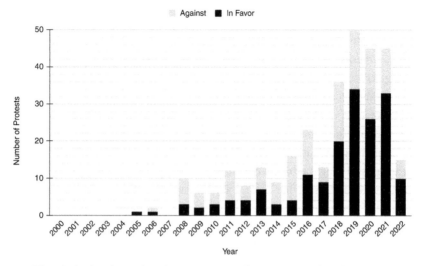

Figure 4 Abortion-related protest events in Latin America since 2000

circulation in eleven Latin American countries.[10] The data suggest that while there was a smattering of social movement activity surrounding abortion from 2005 to 2015, it became a much more salient issue following the growth of feminist mobilization that accompanied NUM in 2015. Initially, there was a relatively even split between pro- and antiabortion activism. But as of 2018, that balance has tilted in favor of abortion rights activists. And beginning in 2018 with Argentina's initial decriminalization bill, the abortion debate in Latin America began in earnest.

In 2020, Argentina legalized abortion in the first fourteen weeks of pregnancy – on the heels of three years of intense mobilization following the initial NUM demonstrations in 2016. In 2021, the Mexican Supreme Court voted to decriminalize abortion, paving the way for full legalization – this decision followed three years of mass mobilization by Mexican women, including a 2020 general strike to demand the state address surging rates of gender violence. In 2022, Colombia decriminalized abortion in the first twenty-four weeks of pregnancy – a victory for social movements like "Causa Justa," which formed in 2017 and became the country's leading abortion rights organization in subsequent years.

---

[10] Argentina (*Clarín* and *La Nación*), Brazil (*Folha de São Paulo* and *O Estado de São Paulo*), Chile (*El Mercurio* and *La Tercera*), Colombia (*El Espectador* and *El Tiempo*), Costa Rica (*La Nación* and *Diario Extra*), El Salvador (*La Prensa Gráfica* and *El Mundo*), Honduras (*El Heraldo* and *La Prensa*), Mexico (*El Universal* and *El Milenio*), Nicaragua (*La Prensa* and *El Nuevo Diario*), Peru (*El Comercio* and *La República*), and Uruguay (*El País* and *La República*).

In our view, the key to understanding recent social progress in one of the most historically conservative regions in the world is mobilization, and abortion is no exception. Beginning with Argentina, feminist social movements throughout the region have adopted similar language and symbols in advocating for reproductive rights, and achieved gains that were once unthinkable. Here we shine a light on the "social movement community" (Staggenborg 1998) that has been forged to advocate for women's interests, and the dual pathways by which reproductive rights have been won: through legislation, and through the courts.

1.3.1 Ni Una Menos and the Making of a Social Movement Community

Ni Una Menos was a campaign to bring attention to gender violence. But it was also the match that would light the flame of a women's movement of unprecedented scope and influence.[11] Soon enough, social movement organizations involved in NUM were advocating for abortion rights. Through linking the movement's claims regarding gender violence to abortion rights, feminist social movements, celebrities, and demonstrators were able to change public opinion and win over powerful political allies, paving the way for legalization in Argentina in 2020. Activists focused on the public health consequences of abortion, and the unequal consequences of prohibition. According to this logic, abortions are going to happen one way or another, but banning them ensures that some women – particularly the poor – will abort in unsafe conditions and die. Without legal abortion, there could be no "ni una menos."

In their efforts to shape public policy and win popular support, social movements adopt frames. Collective action frames are "schemata of interpretation" (Goffman 1974) that are "intended to mobilize potential adherents and constituents, to garner bystander support, and to demobilize antagonists" (Snow and Benford 1988: 198; see also Pedriana 2006; Snow 2013; McAdam 2017). In the case of abortion rights, social movements must craft strategies that turn believers out to rallies, but also be mindful of how to recruit new allies in other social movements, move the needle of public opinion, and persuade political elites who hold the key to reforming the laws on the books.

What has been crucial in Latin America in terms of framing abortion has been altering rights-based frames – similar to the legal arguments that served as the basis for abortion legalization in the United States – to include arguments grounded in notions of social justice. In Uruguay, the successful legalization movement in 2012 broadened the framing of abortion, and "underscored social inequalities regarding access to safe abortions and, therefore, placed the right to

---

[11] We return to *Ni Una Menos* in Section 2, with a more detailed account of that movement's origin in Argentina and its connection to the abortion rights campaign.

abortion (along with its delivery by the public health care system) within the framework of the widening of social rights" (Pousadela 2016: 10). According to Fernández Anderson (2016), this included turning the antiabortion frame on its head by "drawing attention to the maternal deaths due to unsafe abortions and highlighting the disproportionate impact on young and poor women" (10). This approach linked the abortion movement with other social movements focused on issues related to social and economic justice, including gender violence, while highlighting the degree to which poor women in particular suffered from the clandestine nature of the practice.

By May 2016, what began as a movement against femicide and gender violence, which garnered widespread support, had absorbed reproductive rights into the set of claims voiced by a growing social movement community. The grassroots organizing spurred by NUM combined with more formal abortion rights organizations established in the 1980s and 1990s (Lopreite 2012) to form an inclusive and massive abortion rights movement. Furthermore, the social justice framing techniques established in NUM served as a natural "bridge" (Benford and Snow 2000) between gender violence and abortion. By emphasizing the public health dimension of clandestine abortions, the Argentine abortion decriminalization movement leveraged the newly vibrant network of women's organizations to mobilize natural allies, capture the attention of policymakers, and make inroads in changing public opinion.

In Section 2, we discuss the Argentine case in depth, supplementing analysis of survey data with evidence from in-depth interviews of abortion activists. The Argentine case is particularly important, as it inspired the "green wave" protests across the region in 2018. From Chile to Mexico, abortion advocates co-opted the symbolic green scarves worn by Argentine women, and many of the slogans that proved so persuasive in the country's march toward legalization. As Colombian lawyer and abortion rights activist Mariana Ardila put it, "The victories of one country inspire other countries. We share strategies. We talk to each other. We learn from each other" (Otis 2022).

1.3.2 Two Pathways to Legalization

The strategies and frames employed by social movements are shaped by social and political context, or what scholars in contentious politics describe as "political opportunities." Political opportunity structures are "exogenous factors [that] enhance or inhibit prospects for mobilization, for particular sorts of claims to be advanced rather than others, for particular strategies of influence to be exercised, and for movements to affect mainstream institutional politics and policy" (Meyer and Minkoff 2004: 1457–58). In Latin America, two pathways to reform have emerged in recent years: (1) building broad coalitions in legislatures to legalize or loosen restrictions on abortion rights, and (2) legal challenges to the constitutionality of abortion bans that are eventually adjudicated by the Supreme Court.

One key factor shaping whether abortion rights movements can advance their cause through legislatures is the nature and strength of the left party or coalition in government (Blofield and Ewig 2017; Fernández Anderson 2020). Blofield and Ewig (2017) theorize that "institutionalized left" parties are more likely to pass abortion liberalization, compared to "populist left" parties, for the following reasons:

> [W]e find that abortion liberalization proposals are more likely to get on the political agenda and passed in contexts of institutionalized partisan left governance, which has more dispersed party authority. ... By contrast, abortion liberalization proposals are more likely to face rejection (or even reversal) under both populist machine and populist left governments where concentrated, personalist leadership gives feminists fewer opportunities to influence or contest policy. (482)

In contexts like Argentina and Uruguay, where strong left parties (the Peronists or "Partido Justicialista" [PJ] and the Frente Amplio [FA], respectively) encompass diverse coalitions, and have tight connections to civil society, abortion legalization via the legislative process is possible (Fernández Anderson 2020). In the weeks leading up to the legislative debate in Argentina, President Alberto Fernández and his team worked tirelessly to convince undecided senators to support the bill. While the bill eventually passed both houses with supporters (and detractors) from multiple parties, the strength of the PJ was undoubtedly critical in pushing it over the finish line. And the PJ's ties to feminist social movements undoubtedly convinced many prominent politicians, as Vice President (and former president) Cristina Fernández de Kirchner explained: "If you want to know who it was that made me change my mind, it was the thousands of girls who took over the streets. It was seeing them become true feminists" (August 8, 2018).

In Colombia (February 2022) and Mexico (September 2021), abortion rights have been expanded through the courts. Advancing reproductive rights via the judicial path requires a different approach, and is shaped by the amount of support abortion rights movements have in Congress. In Colombia and Mexico, it would be inconceivable that the national legislature would legalize abortion. Yet activists identified several areas where blanket criminalization is inconsistent with civil code. In Colombia, lawyers representing "Causa Justa," a feminist collective, successfully argued that the criminalization of abortion was unjust because many women were unable to access abortion services even when they qualified based on existing law, such as victims of rape. In Mexico, the federal patchwork of abortion laws underlined the legal rationale for justices on the Supreme Court, who overturned a draconian law in Coahuila state that would penalize women who had sought abortions with three years in prison.

Even in cases where it has been the courts, rather than the national legislature, that have made abortion effectively legal, widespread contention has been critical in accelerating the debate. Mexican activists took Argentina's lead, staging numerous mass protests in the months leading up to the Supreme Court decision characterized by masses of green-clad women voicing many of the same rallying cries that were successful in Argentina. On March 8, 2020 – International Women's Day – hundreds of thousands of Mexican women participated in #UnDíaSinNosotras (A Day Without Us), in which they stayed home from work in protest against gender violence.

How have abortion rights movements adapted social movement frames to advance their cause based on the institutional opportunities available to them? In Colombia and Mexico, activists made more technical arguments grounded in Colombia's long history of armed conflict and Mexico's decentralized federal system. That said, the most compelling framing strategy in both countries continued to focus on the devastating public health consequences for poor women, and presented abortion access as a question of social justice. According to this line of argument, as long as clandestine abortions are wide-spread, abortion's illegality only ensures that more poor women die from the procedure:

> These barriers affect mainly women living in (Colombia's) rural and remote areas, low-income women, adolescent girls, women and girls living in situations of armed conflict and victims of gender violence, including physical and sexual violence. (Causa Justa's petition to in the Supreme Court, as quoted in Turkewitz 2022)

> Who will stop a woman – who is desperate to move on with her life project – from interrupting her pregnancy? Reality gives us the answer: neither the dangers associated with a clandestine act, nor society's threats, nor the fear of losing one's life, and much less that of committing a crime. (Justice Yasmín Esquivel, as quoted in Taladrid 2021)

We should note that while Latin America is largely democratic, regimes across the region vary substantially in terms of democratic quality, and countries like Nicaragua and Venezuela have transitioned to illiberal systems of government. Nicaragua and Venezuela represent archetypical examples of populist parties that follow the lead of charismatic authoritarians in Daniel Ortega and Nicolás

Maduro, respectively. Even in such cases where the authoritarian left is in power, without space for public debate and diversity within the governing party, it seems unlikely that abortion rights movements can make their mark.

1.4 Roadmap

The empirical component of this Element begins in Section 2 with a case study of Argentina, a country with a regional legacy of rights expansion and widespread contention (Auyero 2003; Garay 2016; Lapegna 2016; Moseley 2018), that recently legalized abortion in the first fourteen weeks of pregnancy. Argentina offers an illustrative example of the power of social movements, and how abortion activists built on a resonant social movement frame that leveraged political opportunities and won over fellow social movements and Argentine citizens. Argentina represents a "critical case" (Gerring 2004) to evaluate how feminist mobilization successfully placed abortion on the agenda and eventually achieve a ground-breaking legislative victory for Argentine women.

Section 3 takes a comparative approach, analyzing decriminalization movements throughout the Americas. The section begins with Chile, a country where abortion is not yet fully legal, but where restrictions have loosened. We argue that the leftist student movement that emerged in the early 2010s to advocate for educational reform has laid the groundwork for a similar dynamic to what we observe in Argentina. Chilean young people have utilized a familiar social justice frame that has helped grow the movement and persuade bystanders. Following the watershed presidential election victory of Gabriel Boric Font, a former social movement leader, conditions are ripe to incorporate reproductive rights access into an expanding set of progressive claims. We also consider Mexico, a country that has taken the judicial path to decriminalization, and contrast it with the Argentine case.

The case of Nicaragua illustrates a movement to fully criminalize abortion. The country went from legalizing therapeutic abortions to making all abortions illegal in 2006. The law made those who aid in abortion and those who seek out the procedure subject to a prison term of three to ten years. Since the prohibition, public health officials and human rights organizations have documented an increase in the number of deaths from botched abortions. This case enables us to examine the conditions under which we observe an effective movement toward complete abortion criminalization – even in cases of rape or life-threatening pregnancies.

There is a rich literature on the pro-choice and pro-life movements in the United States (e.g., Luker 1985; Staggenborg 1994; Meyer and Staggenborg

2008; Rohlinger 2015). To the extent that an emerging literature on abortion politics in Latin America has dealt with recent activism surrounding reproductive rights, it has centered on institutional actors and their response to mobilization (Fernández Anderson 2020). To our knowledge, no existing study has explored the social movements themselves – that is, inter- and intra-movement organization, perceptions of political opportunities, and framing devices designed to grow their influence and persuade the general public. This entry in the *Cambridge Elements Series in Contentious Politics* builds on previous work by exploring a rapidly changing landscape in abortion rights in Latin America. We argue that mobilization holds the key to understanding reproductive rights expansion in some countries, and retrenchment in others.

2 The Abortion Legalization Movement in Argentina

When Argentina legalized abortion in 2020, it sent shockwaves through Latin America and the rest of the world. It also presented a puzzle for students of abortion rights movements. For a number of reasons, the Argentine case does not seem to fit existing accounts of why such movements emerge, let alone succeed.

The abortion debate materialized in 2018, when the PRO – a right-wing party – governed the country, running contrary to arguments about programmatic left parties being critical to advancing discussions regarding reproductive rights. The leaders of the party, including the president (Mauricio Macri 2015–19), vice president (Gabriela Michetti), and the governor of the province of Buenos Aires (María Eugenia Vidal), did not support legalization. Argentina was not becoming less religious, and public opinion regarding reproductive rights had not changed substantially in the prior decade (AmericasBarometer 2012–17). Indeed, the left-wing governments of the Kirchners (Néstor 2003–7 and Cristina 2007–15) had exited the presidency without opening the discussion for abortion legalization, even when they counted on legislative majorities in Congress. In sum, Argentina was an unlikely place to consider liberalizing abortion laws.

What changed in Argentina to prompt this sudden transformation in terms of abortion policy? We answer this question by focusing on the emergence of a mass feminist movement in 2015 that took to the streets to demand an end to femicide. The appearance of the movement known as NUM ("Not One [Woman] Less") marks a before and after in the history of feminist mobilization in the country. We argue that abortion legalization cannot be understood or explained without NUM. We claim that when a cross-class, inclusive, and transgenerational political movement of women took over the streets in massive numbers in 2015, they changed the landscape of what was possible, transforming the political agenda and, eventually, citizen attitudes and public policy.

We show how Argentine feminists succeeded in translating the power of NUM mobilizations into a campaign for reproductive rights. The argument was simple and straightforward: women could not demand NUM as long as abortion was illegal in the country. Building on the country's tradition of activism for human rights and social justice, feminists built a discourse highlighting disparities in access and safety in abortion practices based on class. Every time a discussion about abortion moved to religious or biological questions, activists brought it back to the fact that women who wanted to have an abortion would have one, so the question was about equality and safety. Feminists demanded legal and safe abortions be performed for free at a public hospital – "educación sexual para decidir, anticonceptivos para no abortar, aborto legal para no morir" (sex education to learn about our bodies, contraception so we do not have abortions, and abortions so we do not die). Centering the debate on class and public health, activists succeeded in mobilizing diverse groups of women across the country to support abortion legalization, and in persuading the uninitiated that legalization was the only path to justice.

2.1 A Brief History of Reproductive Rights in Argentina

The founders of the abortion legalization movement in Argentina experienced the disappearances of many of their friends during the country's brutal military dictatorship in the late 1970s, and several of them went into exile until the return of democracy in 1983. Most of these women were activists in leftist parties and became critical of the country's inattention to gender issues. The experience of being in exile made many aware of gender inequality, and the importance of reproductive rights. The history of Dora Coledesky, the creator of the commission that presented the Law of Abortion Rights in Argentina, is illustrative of the paths of many feminist activists of this generation. Coledesky was a seasoned leftist ("Partido Socialista" and "Partido Obrero").[12] She lived in Tucumán, a small northern province, working in a textile factory where she participated in several strikes and became an elected worker representative. After getting her law degree, she opened a law firm with her husband, but they had to abandon it to go into exile in France in 1976 during the military dictatorship.

While in France, Coledesky, together with other women in exile, began participating in politics, primarily by giving talks about their experience as political exiles. Coledesky learned about feminism and abortion legalization in France and decided to bring those feminist demands to Argentina. Describing

---

[12] Dora Coledesky is self-defined as a Trotskyist.

her years in France, Mabel Belluci, a writer and activist, explains that "Dora became a feminist in France, but not a street feminist . . . she adopted a form of feminism that was institutionalized and academic."[13] When Coledesky returned to Argentina, she resumed her life of activism and, together with her friends and fellow activists, Alicia Schejter, Safina Newbery, María José Rouco Pérez, Laura Bonaparte (historical referent of the Madres de Plaza de Mayo), Carmen González (feminist lawyer), Nadine Osídala, and Rosa Farías (a nurse at Muñiz Hospital) began working to form an organization that would become the first in the country's history to advocate for the right to abortion in Argentina. That group later became known as the "Comisión por el Derecho al Aborto" (Commission for the Right to Abortion, CDA).

Coledesky belonged to a group of leftist women activists who went into exile in Europe and returned to the country as self-discovered feminists. It was the experience of participating in social struggles outside the country that made them feminists. Most of them were classic leftists who interpreted politics primarily through the lens of class, ignoring sex and gender. After their European experiences, they became feminists and participated in politics from that newly acquired position. Dora Coledesky became deeply committed to abortion legalization. These activists, nevertheless, worked primarily within universities and leftist parties, leading to the construction of a less mainstream feminist movement.

Testimonies describe how Coledesky traveled and talked with activists across the country about the importance of legalizing abortion. Most of the activists' campaign was centered on making this issue visible and known to others. Their grassroots work began gaining recognition and visibility several years after, and as Alicia Schejter argued "the fundamental thing was the mobilization of the young girls" ("las pibas"). In an interview examining her historical activism for abortion legalization, Schejter reviewed everything that changed over time, and recognized that the mobilization of young women was the determining factor in explaining the recent changes. "We had been mobilizing since 1988, but what turned things around was the massive mobilization of young women."[14]

One of the spaces where the campaign was developed was in the "Encuentros" (see Figure 5 for a detailed timeline of the major events leading to abortion decriminalization). Following the return of democracy, women began organizing yearly meetings where they met over three days to participate

---

[13] Mabel Bellucci is the author of the book, *Historia de una desobediencia: Aborto y Feminismo* (2019). Coledesky's description and quote was provided by Bellucci in an interview with journalist Juliana Mendoza in *La Nación* (March 7, 2018).

[14] Interview with Alicia Schejter, January 12, 2021. *Prensa Obrera*. This and all subsequent translations from Spanish are by the authors.

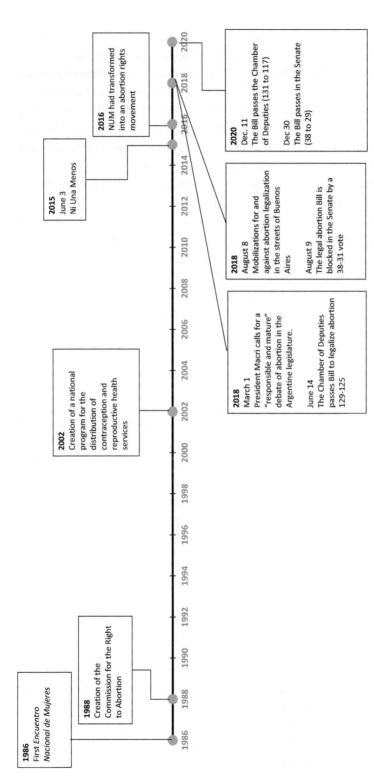

Figure 5 Timeline of the major events leading to abortion decriminalization in Argentina

in different workshops about domestic violence, reproductive rights, labor discrimination, and other important topics for Argentine women. The "Encuentro Nacional de Mujeres" (National Meeting of Women) provided women with a safe space to build community, exchange ideas and practices, and construct and develop a feminist identity (Maffia et al. 2011; Sutton and Borland 2013; Tarducci et al. 2019). The "Encuentros" were critical in introducing and debating international ideas and norms, while providing activists with ideas and narratives to demand policy reform. It was in the "Encuentros" where feminists found a communal space – physically and intellectually – to discuss and develop strategies to campaign for abortion rights.

Drawing from the transnational women's movement for reproductive rights, activists used those ideas and strategies to create, in 2003, a federal plan for the distribution of contraception and other reproductive health services. Yet feminist activists at the time made a conscious decision to frame contraceptive policies as a resource to help prevent poor women from having abortions (Lopreite 2012). Coledesky and other activists saw the campaign for contraception as a trap to put abortion back in the closet; while increased access to contraception marked an important feminist victory in a deeply Catholic nation, it also entrenched abortion as the ultimate taboo topic for meaningful public debate and policy reform.

Abortion rights had always been an issue at the "Encuentros" but did not have national visibility and traction until street activism took over the campaign to pressure politicians and policymakers. This new push to legalize abortion, after years of stalled progress, built from the bottom-up, horizontally, and federally, and succeeded due to the massive street mobilizations that pressured politicians to act. Without the massive feminist mobilizations that accompanied NUM, politicians likely would have continued to place abortion rights on the back-burner, given that most viewed the issue as too polemic and divisive. Before the mobilizations, politicians categorized abortion as an issue that would only reduce their capacity to turn out voters. In 1998, Alberto Maglietti, a former Radical Party senator who authored a bill to decriminalize abortion, said, "No one has demonstrated interest in considering this bill, it is an impolitic issue for the political environment of our country. To speak publicly in favor of abortion is impolitic" (quoted in Htun 2003: 152).

Street mobilizations for abortion legalization forced politicians – as well as journalists, celebrities, and eventually private citizens – to make their positions known. To make abortion mainstream, activists successfully applied a resonant social justice frame to rally allies to their side and win over bystanders. The massive and constant street mobilizations, accompanied by a relentless social media campaign and the unwavering support of many public personalities and celebrities, contributed to the changes in public opinion that resulted in abortion legalization in 2020.

2.2 "Now That They See Us": The Emergence of Ni Una Menos

In 2015, an unprecedented feminist movement swept Argentina. Ni Una Menos was born as a result of the femicide of Chiara Páez. Páez was a fourteen-year-old who was three months pregnant when her boyfriend – with the alleged help of his family – killed and buried her in the family's backyard in Rufino in the province of Santa Fé. A tweet by journalist Marcela Ojeda that read "Actresses, politicians, artists, businesswomen, activists . . . women, all of us, bah, aren't we going to raise our voices? They are killing us" was the match that lit the movement. Páez was neither the first nor the last young Argentine woman to be murdered by her boyfriend, but her case led to the creation of the NUM movement.

The mobilization was organized through social media to call attention to femicides, or the killing of women for being women. Famous soccer players, actors, artists, journalists, athletes, political leaders, NGOs, unions, and influencers used their networks to diffuse the central claim and joined the movement by posting photos of them holding handmade signs with the hashtag #NiUnaMenos. Eventually, there was a call to take to the streets. One day before the mobilization, 71 percent of Argentines were aware of the mobilization, and more than half of the country's adult population (51 percent) said they would participate in the mobilization (Buscaglia 2015).

The first march took place on June 3, 2015, in several cities in Argentina. In the city of Buenos Aires, more than 300,000 women of all ages, races, socioeconomic backgrounds, and political affiliations met in front of the Argentine National Congress to demand state action to stop femicides. Similar marches have followed other high profile femicides that have occurred since, and on June 3 every year, feminist activists have organized massive mobilizations to commemorate the anniversary of the movement.[15]

Once women were in the streets, they became aware of their numbers and began to feel a sense of community. NUM enabled women to think about an "imagined community" (Anderson 1983) of women that was not even a possibility before the mobilization. Many of the attendees went with their grandmothers, mothers, and daughters, demonstrating the intergenerational

---

[15] As evidence of the movement's current prominence in Argentine society, in 2022, current president Alberto Fernández posted a seven-tweet thread on Twitter commemorating the movement, and providing evidence that during his presidency femicides have reached an all-time low.

nature of the mobilization. Beyond differences in age, there were also differences in socioeconomic status and race. Femicides united women in their identity as women; even in a time of high political polarization (known as "la grieta," or "the rift"), women representing and working in different political movements joined with others to demand the end of violence against women. The massive turnout of women from different political groups, levels of education, ages, and socioeconomic status was key to building a movement that would eventually take on abortion rights.

What happened during the mobilization was a reckoning, and the construction of a new massive women's movement that would change politics in the country and the region. Mercedes Funes, one of the movement's organizers, claimed that the main transformation was that women began "recognizing themselves as a collective subject with an enormous force to install gender issues on the political, media, and social agenda."[16] In 2015, only academics and policymakers knew the term "femicide," and there were no official registries. Nowadays, while data collection continues to be fraught, everyone in Argentina and the region knows the meaning of the term "femicide," demonstrating the NUM movement's tremendous impact.

Beyond Argentina, NUM mobilizations took place in most countries in Latin America, as women across the region echoed Argentine women's call to end violence against women. NUM mobilizations experienced a powerful process of diffusion that has had a profound effect on domestic politics in countries throughout the region. The same movements that replicated the Argentine NUM would later follow Argentina's lead once again in demanding abortion legalization, albeit with mixed results.

2.2.1 An Inclusive Feminist Movement

A strength of the movement was its inclusivity. The movement welcomed every woman to join, and the streets displayed this variation in social class, race, and age in every mobilization. Women from the poorest areas marched together with those from the wealthiest neighborhoods. Brown and white women were on the streets together, along with women who supported all political parties ranging from the right to the left. The movement was profoundly political but not partisan. Indeed, there were no partisan signs at the demonstrations, as violence against women was not presented as a partisan issue. Moreover, political parties everywhere were catching up with a grassroots movement that demanded politicians act on an issue they were unwilling to act upon before the mobilizations.

---

[16] Interview of Merecedes Funes by Clara Fernández Escudero (*Perfil*, June 3, 2020).

Several of the participants went to the streets with their group of friends, but others chose to do it with their families. It was not unusual to see groups of three or four generations of women marching together – adding to the emotional component of the mobilizations.

> Being there with my grandma, my mom, and my daughter, it's hard, almost impossible to describe. It was a feeling of union, communion, love, gratitude. I was also angry, but hopeful. Angry that we [women] have to be on the streets demanding our rights. For rights that we should have had for years. Hopeful for my daughter's generation, for seeing my grandma and mom see the power of women together, something that I don't think either of them thought they would ever see.[17]

The inclusivity of the movement and its massive character led to the construction of a community that, once seen and heard, could not be invisible and muted again. Eventually, women were on the streets demanding their right to free and safe abortions, and the world was watching.

Class differences were also present and visible at the mobilizations. It was clear to those participating that both wealthy and poor women attended the mobilizations. Several wealthy women whose children attended the most exclusive private English, German, Italian, and French schools in the country and those in private universities were there, sometimes together with their children, and sometimes with friends. Next to them, there were women from popular shantytown organizations. Whereas before NUM and the mobilizations to legalize abortion, it would have been hard to imagine what these women have in common, their experiences with gender discrimination and, for many of them, domestic violence and illegal abortions unified them.

Our interviews as well as written and media testimonies from the mobilizations document the presence of women from Recoleta (one of the most exclusive neighborhoods in Buenos Aires), working-class neighborhoods (poor areas of José C. Paz, San Miguel, Malvinas Argentinas, and Pilar), and several shantytowns (see, for instance, the presence of the shantytown movement "La Garganta Poderosa"). When mobilizations took place on work days, women also attended together with those who worked for them, illustrating the inclusive nature of the movement and the demand:

> The day of the march, my mother and I were going to go, and I told my mom that we should invite Lidia, the woman who cleans our house. We knew that Lidia agreed with us about all of this, because we had discussed femicides and domestic violence with her. When we asked her, initially she said that she needed to finish cleaning and my mom replied, "Forget about that!" and she

---

[17] Author interview, December 2018.

came with us. I'm conscious of privilege and class differences, and I'm aware that there aren't a lot of moments when the three of us would all march together for the same cause. It was wonderful. I will never forget it.[18]

College students from different social classes worked together for abortion legalization. When we attended community meetings with university students where discussions about abortion legalization took place, it became apparent that several activists did not have much in common regarding class and partisanship. However, they were nevertheless working together to achieve gender equity and eventually, reproductive rights. Educated university students were aware of their differences and chose systematically to focus on their "shared oppression due to their gender." "It really doesn't matter who your parents are, how much money you have, where you live. None of us can have an abortion. Period. We all want the same. That's it. It's that simple."[19]

2.2.2 The Revolution of the Daughters

Feminism has become a potent political force in the region. In many of our conversations with teenagers and young women, feminism appeared as the driving reason for them to enter the political arena. "I had never been into politics or mobilizations. I didn't feel any of the existing grievances were mine until this."[20] Feminism became a political movement that united women in the region and enabled the entrance into politics of a new generation of young girls and women who identified as feminists. Journalist and activist Luciana Peker describes this phenomenon as "the revolution of the daughters" ("la revolucion de las hijas").

Describing the scene in the streets while Congress was discussing the abortion bill in the lower chamber, a well-known activist told us: "I looked around me, and I knew we won. Most of those around me were teenagers."[21] Women, especially young women, were the core of mobilizations in Argentina and other Latin American countries. They were central in displaying costumes and creative art and using their voices to chant clever songs supporting abortion legalization. They also signified how when it came to reproductive rights in Latin America, times were changing.

A famous writer and activist in Buenos Aires told us that she had not found something that made her identify with her country before the women's mobilization. People commented about tango and soccer every time she traveled, two things in which she had no interest. Feminism and street mobilizations were the first

---

[18] Author interview, December 2018.   [19] Author interview, December 2018.

[20] Author interview, April 2022.

[21] Author's phone conversation with an activist participating in the mobilization in front of the Congress building during the day of the congressional vote.

things that made her proud of her nationality. "Talking about my country as one in which women fight on the streets for their rights, that really made me proud."[22]

Young women made an impression on political elites as well. The highest profile was former president Cristina Fernández de Kirchner, who explained why she changed her mind from opposing abortion while she was president to voting in favor of its legalization when she was a national senator. In her biographical book, *Sincerely* (2019), as well as in her speech in Congress during the hours-long legislative debate, Fernández de Kirchner explained the impact that the mobilizations, especially the massive turnout of young women (including her daughter) in the streets had in changing her mind.

> I think that more than a gender issue, this is a generational issue. The kids, once again, make the rest of us aware of the change of time and demand to be heard. If you want to know who made me change my mind, it was the thousands and thousands of girls who took to the streets. Seeing them address the feminist question, seeing them criticize, but also describe the reality of a patriarchal society should take all of us to a different place.

Fernández de Kirchner reflected that it was not only her daughter who made her change her mind, but high school students and thinking about how she was going to be seen years later by her granddaughters.

> I wracked my brain thinking about those girls [13-, 14- and 15-year-olds] and then my daughter started sending me photos of the school takeovers, and I started to think . . . in fifteen years I am going to be 80, I'm going to be an old woman and Helenita [granddaughter] is going to be in the fifth year, María Emilia [granddaughter] is going to be a senior in high school, and their classmates are going to ask them: "Hey, what did your grandmother vote for?" And they are going to answer: "That old woman voted against." No, sir! . . . I'm not going to allow that. No, no, no, no way. I am not willing to be remembered badly by my granddaughters. I definitely don't want that.

The feminist movement has been a source of hope for many in a context where politics and economics are disastrous. In our last field trip in April 2022, amid a political and economic crisis, most of our interviewees agreed that the feminist movement, and the legalization of abortion, was one of, if not the only, positive things to happen in the country in years.

2.2.3 The Legacy of Nunca Más

It is impossible to write about the history of the women's movement in Argentina without mentioning the "Madres de la Plaza de Mayo" (Mothers of

---

[22] Author interview, April 2022.

the Plaza de Mayo). During the dictatorship, a group of mothers whose children had been kidnapped and disappeared decided to organize. Mothers searching for their children and grandmothers searching for their grandchildren, who were kidnapped by the military and handed over to adoptive families, shared their desperation to know the whereabouts of their loved ones. They began organizing to share resources and meet weekly on Thursdays at the pyramid in the Plaza de Mayo (in front of the government house) to demand the appearance ("aparición con vida") of their disappeared children. Many of the women, including the movement's founders, had not had any political experience or participation before the disappearances of their family members. Using their nonpolitical social role as mothers, they politicized their motherhood role as caregivers of their missing children (Noonan 1995).

The Mothers' role was central in delegitimizing the authoritarian regime and resurrecting a civil society that was afraid and dormant during the dictatorship (O'Donnell et al. 1986). They became an iconic and internationally recognized human rights group, as did the white handkerchiefs they wore on their heads.[23] The idea of the white handkerchiefs was symbolic and practical. To identify themselves, they decided to cover their heads with cloth diapers that many of them used in taking care of their grandchildren whose parents had been kidnapped and disappeared.

Building on the Madres' tradition of being political but not partisan, women in the abortion movement chose to use the same handkerchief that the "Madres" and "Abuelas" used to self-identify themselves. The movement for abortion legalization borrows from this tradition by using a different color: green. Many of the cartoons and graphic images used during the campaign showed images of a young woman wearing a green handkerchief and a grandmother wearing a white one with slogans reading: "today and forever."

Actresses, writers, and journalists wore the green handkerchiefs on prime-time television programs, shows, and awards ceremonies. Most importantly, young girls, especially high school and college students, wore them on their backpacks. As a result, it became common to observe young girls and adults signaling pro-abortion beliefs on public transport and on the streets. Women, girls, and activists throughout Latin America adopted this symbol to fight for abortion rights in their countries. Recently in the United States, activists protesting the overturn of Roe vs. Wade have worn the same green handkerchiefs that Argentine feminists made famous, including Congresswoman Alexandra Ocasio-Cortez.

---

[23] Over time, the use and meaning of the handkerchiefs changed. Madres de Plaza de Mayo did an interesting documentary where they asked different members about the meaning of those handkerchiefs after forty-three years. See www.youtube.com/watch?v=0nx7ZylORto.

2.3 From Ni Una Menos to Abortion Rights

How did the NUM movement become a transformative force to legalize abortion? Abortion had not been discussed much in public in Argentina before. There were feminist activists who sought abortion legalization, but the issue, in the words of a former senator who authored a bill to decriminalize the practice, was "impolitic."[24] Politicians saw abortion as an issue that reduced political capital ("pianta votos"), and thus it was never considered. We show how the NUM movement contributed to the transition from impolitic to political.

2.3.1 Mobilizing a Massive Social Movement Community for Abortion Rights

The NUM movement provided a massive organizational base to demand abortion legalization. Participants in the campaign built an organizational structure that helped the abortion rights movement overcome classic collective action problems (Zald and Ash 1966; McCarthy and Zald 1977). This collective included celebrities, famous writers, actresses, and organized groups of women from different places and backgrounds – labor unions, shantytowns, lawyers, advocacy groups – and young women, mostly from universities and public and private high schools. Many of those who participated in NUM were proficient in using social networks to share information. Since the NUM movement began, there was a shift in existing unwritten norms and culture that led women to believe there was space to demand change.

This transition from NUM to abortion rights mobilization brings to mind work on how campaigns build on one another, expanding social movement "communities" surrounding a given issue area (Staggenborg 1988; Staggenborg and Lecomte 2009). In Argentina, new women's "agrupaciones" (collectives) joined established organizations in the campaign to end gender violence, and the linkages between those groups would persist beyond NUM. According to Tilly (2008), campaigns are "a sustained, coordinated series of episodes involving similar claims on similar or identical targets" (89). A campaign can affect future campaigns when it "transforms political opportunity structure, changes the array of available models for contentious performances, and alters connections among potential actors" (89).

With NUM, the creation of a massive social movement community surrounding women's issues satisfied all of Tilly's core criteria for shaping future campaigns. The campaign against gender violence created new political opportunities to bring attention to women's issues. The mass demonstrations in front

---

[24] See Htun's interview (2003: 152) with Alberto Maglieti.

of the National Congress, and in city centers across the country, where activists were united in terms of their messaging in "cantitos" (songs), symbolic garb, and radical performances of womanhood altered the repertoire of performances available to women's social movements.

The mix of established advocacy organizations and new insurgent collectives forged during NUM was a potent one. NUM combined veteran social movement organizations like the "Fundación para el Estudio y la Investigación de la Mujer" (FEIM; Foundation for the Study and Research of Women), which was founded in 1989 and has advocated for contraceptive access and against gender violence for decades. FEIM has formally supported abortion decriminalization since 2005 – long before it was a prominent issue in Argentine politics and society (Uranga 2018). Yet new movements, largely composed of younger, more radical feminists, also played a critical role in building NUM (Daby and Moseley 2022). "Mala Junta" formed in 2015 amid the rise of NUM and represents the embodiment of "popular feminism," focused on combating neoliberal policies more broadly, including Argentina's prohibition on abortion, which disproportionately penalizes poor women. Other groups, such as MuMaLá (Mujeres de la Matría Latinoamericana), were tied to left political parties like "Libres de Sur."

Ni Una Menos first appeared in 2015. Within a year, the movement had absorbed abortion into its set of demands, setting the stage for another campaign to pursue abortion rights. Before the mobilization planned to mark the one-year anniversary of NUM, abortion rights appeared for the first time in an official NUM manifesto on the organization's website:

> When a young woman is imprisoned in Tucumán, condemned to eight years in prison for homicide when she had a miscarriage, in a fraudulent case, it obligates us to reiterate the claim that without legalized abortion, there is no "Ni Una Menos," and go back to the streets with more resolve than ever before. To machista violence and those who would perpetrate it, we say: Ni Una Menos, and against our bodies, Never Again. (Ni Una Menos website, May 9, 2016)

By 2016, the NUM campaign against gender violence had transformed into an abortion rights campaign. As Figure 6 shows, street demonstrations surrounding abortion experienced a fairly steady uptick from 2015 to 2020, setting the stage for the vote in Congress. This is a direct consequence of NUM. The organizational complexity that feminist activists had built in protesting against gender violence was thrown behind abortion rights, grounded in the notion that illicit, clandestine abortion itself was an act of violence against women – "without legalized abortion, there is no 'ni una menos.'" Some folks who

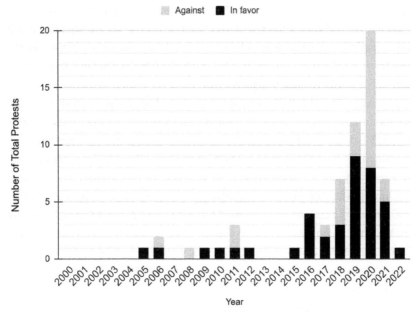

Figure 6 Abortion protests over time in Argentina (2000–22)

initially supported the claims against femicide undoubtedly defected when abortion rights were brought into the fold. But many new activists who had never viewed abortion as a question of social justice were persuaded to continue mobilizing for reproductive rights.

It is no coincidence that the first real vote on abortion legalization in Congress occurred in 2018, following two years of intense mobilization. Argentina has had gender quotas since the early 1990s and elected a woman president in 2007; the center-left Peronist Party governed the country from 2003 to 2015 and passed important progressive legislation to address LGBTQ+ rights and reduce poverty. But it took hundreds of thousands of women in the streets to push policymakers to consider legalizing abortion. What changed in Argentina was the emergence of a massive social movement community, armed with a rallying cry that would resonate with the Argentine public and policymakers alike.

2.3.2 An Old Frame Takes on New Resonance

Ni Una Menos planted the seeds for building a massive social movement community surrounding women's issues, and a unique platform to link reproductive rights to gender violence. While abortion, along with other issues like access to contraception (Lopreite 2012; Sutton and Borland 2013), had long been framed in terms of social justice in Argentina, NUM provided a window of opportunity for the abortion rights movement to deliver its message to a much larger audience. Social justice claims have a deep, entrenched history in the country. It is a resonant framework that social movements and labor unions have used successfully to achieve rights.

The Argentine feminist movement framed abortion as inseparable from economic inequality and gender violence, thus piggybacking on the success of NUM. Frames of collective action are "schemata of interpretation" (Goffman 1974) "intended to mobilize potential adherents and constituents, to garner bystander support, and to demobilize antagonists" (Snow and Benford 1988: 198; see also Pedriana 2006; Snow 2013; McAdam 2017). Building on the country's tradition of advocacy, and the recent gains made by NUM in mobilizing women to take to the streets, Argentine feminists framed abortion as an issue of social and economic justice. The argument was simple: poor women die due to clandestine abortions. Without legal abortion, there could be no "ni una menos." Avoiding philosophical questions about the origins of life or discussions about the fetus's viability and legal justifications about women's rights to privacy, Argentine feminists used empirical evidence to advance their cause. "In countries where abortion is illegal, many women undergo the procedure in clandestine circumstances at great risk to their health. Complications from botched abortions are a leading cause of maternal mortality in many countries and produce a major drain on the public health system" (Htun 2003: 142).

"Las ricas abortan, las pobras mueren" (The rich have abortions, the poor die) was repeated by all of those who supported legalization. Every time someone on TV, radio, or even in the streets argued that they were saving lives – referring to the unborn – activists pointed out that lives would be lost due to illegality. The simplicity of the argument was to bring the conversation back to the reality that women who want to have an abortion will get one. The question was if the state would make sure they do it in safe conditions. As one of the "cantitos" (songs) performed on the streets stated: "aborto legal, en el hospital" (legal abortions in hospitals). Framing abortion as a social justice issue complicated the positions of those who sought to keep the practice illegal because facts made crystal clear that wealthy women have safe abortions, while poor women die. Endorsing criminalization meant complicity in codifying a pernicious consequence of social inequality. Antiabortion activists never found a way to deal with the wealth of statistics indicating how mostly poor women died due to illegal abortions. More than half (54 percent) of low-income women are likely to have an unsafe abortion instead of 1 percent of higher-income and 5 percent of upper-middle-income women (Singh et al. 2018).

This framing of abortion rights as intrinsically tied to economic inequality and social justice was not new. It echoed prior messaging strategies employed by women's groups in Argentina to expand access to contraception: "The rationale for adopting new contraceptive policies was framed primarily as a way to help poor women. ... In countries with a weak tradition of civil rights, the focus on health, poverty and inequality may provide a strategic option for seeking [abortion] reforms [compared to rights-based arguments], especially as they face strong organized opposition." (Lopreite 2012: 124)

What was new was the reach of the message, now ringing out from massive demonstrations across the country (and on social media) in the new post-NUM era, buoyed by the support of a diverse and inclusive social movement community. NUM signified a sea change in terms of the political opportunities available for abortion rights activists to reach new audiences, and make Argentines consider the degree to which unsafe clandestine abortion and gender violence were one in the same, particularly for poor women.

By rooting abortion in a social justice framework, the feminist movement anchored the movement for abortion decriminalization in a history of street-based activism to promote economic justice. It also provided women from all social classes a sense of community that enabled the construction of solidarity, making "it easier to face the risks and uncertainties of collective action" (Diani and Della Porta 2005: 95). Grounding advocacy for abortion decriminalization in a social justice framework, activists tapped a resonant frame for the Argentine context focusing on the socioeconomic dimensions of abortion (Ferree 2003). The campaign was that abortion should be legal, safe, and free ("aborto legal, seguro, y gratuito").

The movement was successful in shifting public opinion in favor of legalization. It is important to note that significant shifts in terms of public opinion occurred *after* the mobilizations in the street. As Figure 6 shows, street protests for abortion rights reemerged in 2016, on the heels of NUM, and by 2018 had kicked into high gear. Figure 7 illustrates how the greatest shift in terms of public support for abortion rights occurred from 2017 to 2019, when levels of abortion justification increased from 64 to 72 percent. According to data from the AmericasBarometer, this sea change in terms of public opinion was most pronounced *among men*, who reported a ten-point increase in acceptance of abortion when the mother's life is at risk from 2017 to 2019 (Figure 7).

In 2018, as Congress prepared to debate the first bill to decriminalize abortion (which would fail in the Senate), abortion activists knew they had changed the conversation regarding reproductive rights for good: "We already won. Today we don't vote for abortion "yes," abortion "no," but legal abortion or

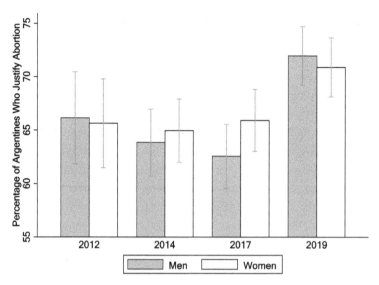

Figure 7 Abortion justification in Argentina over time
(AmericasBarometer 2019)

clandestine abortion. Each new death due to clandestine abortion will be the responsibility of the senators who vote against legalization today." (Lucía Sánchez, a high school student; Centenera 2018)

2.3.3 A Countermovement Emerges: *"Salvemos Las Dos Vidas"*

Following the materialization of a full-fledged abortion rights movement, which piggybacked on NUM and had widespread support by 2018, green handkerchief-clad abortion activists outnumbered any competing political force in the streets of Buenos Aires and other major cities throughout the country. In early 2018, President Macri announced that he supported a "responsible and mature" debate regarding abortion rights, to the dismay of many of his conservative allies across the country.[25] In the months that followed, a group of proabortion legislators brought forward the "Ley de Interrupción Legal del Embarazo" (ILE), which would legalize abortion through the first twelve weeks of pregnancy. The legislation passed in the Chamber of Deputies, and was sent to the Senate, which experts on legislative politics in Argentina suspected was the real obstacle to full legalization.

---

[25] Macri's motivations have been the subject of considerable debate among scholars of Argentine politics. The more generous explanations sustain that Macri's openness to dialogue reflected a principled, democratic willingness to listen to arguments and be persuaded. The less generous and pragmatic explanations highlight that he found in abortion a distraction from the dire economic conditions in the country.

The possibility that Argentina might legalize abortion served as a wake-up call for conservatives, spurring the emergence of a prominent countermovement: "Salvemos Las Dos Vidas" (Let's save both lives). Meyer and Staggenborg (1996) define countermovements as "networks of individuals and organizations that share many of the same objects of concern as the social movements they oppose. They make competing claims on the state on matters of policy and politics . . . and vie for attention from the mass media and broader public" (1632).

According to Meyer and Staggenborg, movements generate countermovements to the extent that they "first . . . show signs of success; second, the interests of some population are threatened by movement goals; and third, political allies are available to aid oppositional mobilization" (1635). The rise of a viable legalization movement, and clear evidence that feminist activists were having some success in recruiting powerful allies in positions of power, represented a warning sign to conservative Argentines. The Argentine antiabortion movement drew heavily on the support of Argentine Catholics, as major figures of the church in the country urged their fellow believers to take to the streets and defend the rights of the unborn. Movement adherents appealed to nationalism in their choice to adopt Argentina's light blue ("celeste") as their symbolic adornment.

On August 8, 2018, antiabortion activists called on Argentines to flood the streets of Buenos Aires to protest the ILE decriminalization bill under consideration in the Argentine Senate. Abortion rights activists countered by calling their own supporters to defend women's right to control their own bodies. The #8A rally in Buenos Aires offered a stark illustration of the polarization surrounding abortion rights that had crystallized in recent years. In anticipation of the event, the government undertook massive security measures to close off twenty-eight streets near Congress for the green wave protests, and twenty-one for the light blue wave activists (Centenera 2018).

On August 9, 2018, the Senate rejected the ILE legislation, and antiabortion activists could breathe a sigh of relief. But there was a palpable sense that the abortion rights movement had achieved something akin to the "social decriminalization" of abortion (Tarducci 2018: 430). An abortion decriminalization bill had never made it so far in Congress, and the tens of thousands of women in the streets of Buenos Aires on the day the Senate rendered its vote proved that the abortion debate would continue in Argentina.

2.4 Abortion Legalization in Argentina

When the 2018 bill was narrowly defeated in the Argentine Senate, it did not mean the abortion debate was over. If anything, abortion rights activists doubled down, sensing that electing a new government in 2019 with friendlier views toward the insurgent feminist movement in Argentina could tip the scales in legalization's favor. Incumbent president Macri of the center-right "Cambiemos" (Let's Change) coalition appeared vulnerable amidst an ongoing economic crisis, which meant that abortion rights activists needed only to win over the Peronist ticket to have a good chance at passing abortion legislation.

With the 2019 presidential election approaching, the notoriously fractious Peronist Party convened to choose a ticket that would unite the progressive wing of the party, led by Fernández de Kirchner, and the more centrist wing of the party, with its deep ties to provincial political machines. The compromise was a ticket that featured Alberto Fernández, former cabinet head for Néstor Kirchner and PJ stalwart, at the top of the ticket, and Fernández de Kirchner as his running mate. In August of 2019, Fernández stated that he was in favor of abortion rights, but given the depth of the economic crisis in the country, did not view it as a legislative priority. He argued that first, Argentina must decriminalize abortion, and stop punishing women for seeking out abortion services. Then, he argued, they could open the debate on legalization, in which the state would take responsibility for carrying out abortions.

Yet pressure mounted within the new "Frente de Todos" (Everybody's Front) coalition, which counted on the support of party factions and civil society organizations to Fernández's left, to take a stronger stance on the topic. Finally, after a decisive victory in the first-round election, Fernández gave abortion activists the ringing endorsement that they wanted in October 2019, only weeks before the second round of the presidential election:

> I'm not going to escape the abortion issue, everyone knows what I think.
> Continuing to punish it, the only thing it does is criminalize the practice and
> make everything clandestine. We must move towards legalization, because
> with legalization we are going to give poor women the opportunity to have
> their abortions in safe conditions just like the rich do in the big sanatoriums.
> Let's put an end to hypocrisy.[26]

Fernández's position on abortion – which echoed the resonant framing deployed by the feminist movement in recent years – stood in stark contrast to Macri's rhetoric in the weeks leading up to the election. Fernández made public his position to legalize abortion during the electoral campaign. Following a decisive defeat in the primary elections, which serve as something of a straw poll in Argentina, Macri's Cambiemos coalition took a stronger stance on abortion, banking on a perceived hesitancy among Argentines to give

---

[26] In a radio interview, Alberto Fernández insisted with this line of argument: "Abortions are clandestine. It is a public health issue and it needs to be resolved. We cannot continue to be hypocrites, once and for all we must stop putting the lives of young women at risk" (as quoted in *Infobae*, October 26, 2019).

abortion the green light. Both Macri and incumbent governor of Buenos Aires María Eugenia Vidal appeared at antiabortion rallies with light blue handkerchiefs, and proclaimed in a number of public events that they were in favor of "saving both lives" and rejected abortion legalization.

Record turnout swept the Peronists back into the "Casa Rosada" after only a four-year absence. But this time, the party had a mandate to make abortion legalization a central component of its legislative project. Upon taking office, Fernández promised to introduce a bill that would legalize abortion, along with another bill called the "1000-day plan" that would boost state support for women during pregnancy, childbirth, and in the first few years of their children's lives. On abortion, Fernández echoed the well-honed framing of activists who focused on social justice and public health in justifying his plan:

> What we have to solve is a public health problem, that the woman who aborts [in unsafe clandestine conditions] puts her life at risk.
>
> This has to do with Argentine hypocrisy ... Many times, those who abort are daughters of wealthy families who go to mass but cannot bear the disgrace of having a single daughter with a son. Let's end the hypocrisy. The woman who wants to abort, is going to abort, and the one who wants to have a child, let her have it. And let's give her the conditions so that her kid lives happily in the world. (as quoted in *Clarín* 2019)

On November 17, 2020, Fernández sent a new version of the ILE legislation to the Chamber of Deputies, and requested that both houses of Congress vote on abortion legalization prior to the end of the year. On December 10, the legislation passed in the Chamber of Deputies by a 131–117 vote – close to the final tally in favor of legalization in 2018. But the Senate was still the major hurdle, given its overrepresentation of conservative interior provinces. The president and his cabinet worked with hesitant senators to revise the content of the legislation, and by December 29, it appeared that the government had the votes it needed to pass legalized abortion into law.

On the sultry summer night of December 30, 2020, tens of thousands of abortion rights activists gathered in front of the National Congress in anticipation of the Senate's final vote. When the final result of 38–29 in favor of legalization aired on the big screen in the plaza facing Congress, the green-clad activists responded with jubilation. Ultimately, the government's co-partisans supported legalization at a higher rate, but a number of legislators from the opposition "Cambiemos" voted for the ILE. While 68 percent of female senators voted for legalization, only 43 percent of male senators approved the ILE.

In Argentina, mobilization had made the difference in achieving legal abortion. Building on NUM, the abortion rights movement leveraged a massive social movement community and resonant framing to finally bring abortion into mainstream politics. More than three decades after Dora Coledesky created the Commission for the Right to Abortion, abortion was finally law in Argentina.

3 A Green Wave? Diverging Pathways toward Rights Expansion and Retrenchment

Feminist movements in Latin America have pursued different paths to achieve abortion legalization, with varying degrees of success. In Argentina and Uruguay, feminist movements pursued a legislative strategy, lobbying legislators and policymakers. In Colombia and Mexico, feminists achieved decriminalization through the Supreme Court. In Chile, feminists are trying to achieve legalization by including reproductive rights in a new constitution. Our research documents how activists pursue multiple paths simultaneously: feminist lawyers work on legal cases to bring to courts, feminist political activists lobby legislators and policymakers, and feminist journalists, writers, and celebrities aim to persuade the public over social and mass media. While pursuing multiple paths simultaneously, activists are aware that some paths are likelier to be viable than others.

The legislative path, which we cover extensively in Section 2 on Argentina, is promising when activists are able to build broad public support in the streets and power via the ballot box, eventually enabling proabortion movements to construct a coalition of legislators willing to publicly support abortion legalization. The judicial path requires progressive courts that are receptive to feminist claims and likely to advance reproductive rights. Based on the literature, those courts would need to be independent, progressive (in the theory of jurisprudence they follow), and open to transnational legalism in evaluating claims to extend reproductive rights (Halliday and Shaffer 2015; Corrales 2021). The judicial path has been used to advance sexual and reproductive rights, same-sex marriage, and abortion. Similar to the legislative path, one of the most important conditions for successful judicialization in advancing abortion rights is the presence of a massive and inclusive feminist movement on the streets that demands and supports these judicial measures. Having progressive courts without "mass-based activism and effective public outreach strategies" truncates the "rights-affirming promise of judicialization" (Botero et al. 2022: 23).

This section examines three different cases in the region: Chile, Mexico, and Nicaragua. In Chile, abortion was illegal under all circumstances until 2017 (divorce was legalized only in 2004, and same-sex marriage in 2021). After the "estallido social" (the 2019 Chilean uprising), social movements, especially those led by high school and college students, have been protagonists in changing the country. The election of President Gabriel Boric, a thirty-five-year-old former student leader, illustrates these changes. Recognizing the importance of the feminist movement, in 2022 Boric named the most female cabinet in Latin American history. As a result years of mobilization, Chile is rewriting its constitution, and will be the first country in the world with a constitutional convention that features full gender parity. If the right to abortion is approved, it could be constitutionally protected – a step beyond even the legislative victories won by abortion rights movements in Argentina and Uruguay.

Mexico is a case that illustrates how activists can achieve decriminalization through the judicial path. In 2021, due to differences across states in abortion law, the Supreme Court decriminalized abortion. Before the ruling, Mexican women had different access to abortion, and faced different penalties, based on where they lived. The Supreme Court's ruling recognized this disparity in its decision to decriminalize abortion. The Court's ruling also encourages states to expand the conditions and the length of time during which women can access abortions. It is, nevertheless, up to each state to decide. Rape, however, is a condition under which women have access to abortion at any time in all Mexican states.

Finally, the case of Nicaragua exemplifies a set of cases in which the movement to retrench abortion rights has been effective. In 2006, Nicaragua went from allowing abortions on therapeutic grounds to banning all abortions. Nicaragua demonstrates how governments can retrench existing reproductive rights for women when they align with religious groups due to ideological overlap or for political gain. Examining Nicaragua's push to ban all abortion sheds light on the trajectories of other Central American and Caribbean countries, while revealing how the absence of a robust feminist movement enables these retrenchments.

Independent of which path each country takes, all of them benefit from the support of feminists on the streets. When mobilizations are massive and turnout is inclusive and representative of women's diverse population in each country, their demands are likely to become visible (Weldon 2006). Visibility creates new political opportunities for abortion rights groups to disseminate their message to a larger audience and carve out space on the policy agenda, as parties and courts scramble to respond to demands made at street demonstrations and in popular media. As our data show, mobilization tends to *precede* substantial changes in terms of public opinion, and in contexts where movements make inroads in convincing the public, they can eventually reach political elites.

The dominant framing of abortion among movements that have achieved meaningful gains in terms of reproductive rights in the region is that abortion is about social justice. When abortion is illegal, poor women die. If women want an abortion, they will get one – the only way policymakers and judges can make a positive difference in women's lives is by making sure those who choose to abort do so under safe conditions.

The most effective movements have also been successful in mobilizing a diverse collective of women across socioeconomic backgrounds, especially young women, to participate *together* in politics for the first time. As several of the testimonies we collected for this project show, a sizable number of high school and college students who had not participated or been interested in politics before, felt called by the feminist movement. While at the beginning of the mobilizations, many of them did not know much about feminism, and would not have identified as feminists, learning about their own history and building a community changed their identity in profound ways. Many young women told us that while they did not identify with one political party in particular, they all identified with feminism.

When NUM emerged, and then provided the framework for an abortion rights campaign across Latin America, the politics surrounding the issue changed fundamentally. Regardless of the variation in outcomes, it is important to highlight that the feminist movement succeeded in taking abortion out of the closet. Women now talk publicly about having had an abortion, about going to clandestine clinics, about their fear, about their sense of loneliness. The destigmatization of abortion has also led societies to become more aware of the extent of the practice. Many men have learned that their spouse, partner, mother, sister, or friend had an abortion. Public and private discussions about abortion became possible, removing abortion from the category of taboo, "impolitic" topics. This, in itself, has constituted an important victory for the feminist movement.

3.1 The Long Road to Abortion Rights in Chile

The history of abortion legalization in Chile exemplifies a nonlinear trajectory toward legalization (see Figure 8 for a detailed timeline of the major events leading to discussions of abortion legalization). While the country has had provisions that enabled abortions in some instances since 1931, the dictatorship of Augusto Pinochet (1973–90) made the practice illegal under any circumstances. When Chile transitioned to democracy in 1990, some coalition parties of the "Concertación de Partidos por la Democracia" (a broad, center-left coalition) tried to expand abortion access. However, the strength and preferences of some parties within the governing coalition complicated those efforts. Only in her second government was President Michele Bachelet (2006–10) able to decriminalize therapeutic abortions.

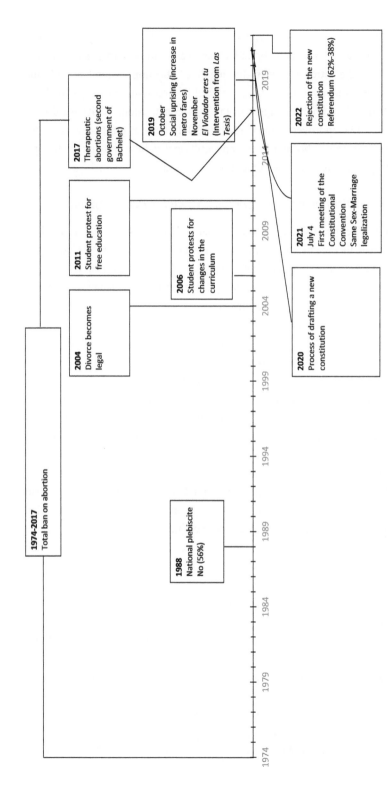

Figure 8 Timeline of the major events leading to discussions about abortion legalization in Chile

The current government of President Gabriel Boric (elected in 2022), with its strong ties to social movements and extensive feminist participation in the cabinet and the streets, seeks to legalize abortion. Members of the Constitutional Convention, which is the world's first with gender parity, have proposed including abortion rights in the new constitution. While we do not know if it will be approved when Chile ultimately decides on its new constitution, the inclusion of abortion in the constitutional debate shows the strength and efficacy of the feminist movement in the country.

3.1.1 Dictatorship and Reproductive Rights Retrenchment

Abortion was defined as a crime in the penal code of 1874. However, in 1931, exceptions for therapeutic purposes were established in the Health Code. This exception was maintained until 1989, when the military dictatorship of Augusto Pinochet criminalized all types of voluntary termination of pregnancies. Women's movements were central in questioning the regime's legitimacy and contributed to Chile's eventual transition to democracy. During Chile's brutally repressive military regime, victims' wives, sisters, mothers, and daughters became politicized and demanded to know about their loved ones and those left behind. The authoritarian government forced them to assume "a triple role: caretaker of the home and children, economic provider for the family, and caretaker of the community" (Noonan 1995: 100). Studying political opportunities and collective action frames in Chile's transition to democracy, Noonan (1995) finds that women's politicization eventually transformed from a maternal to a feminist frame.

Women's organizations were also key actors in the "No" campaign during the 1988 plebiscite to decide whether Pinochet would continue in power. Their slogan was "We want democracy in the country, and at home."[27] The authoritarian government's actions contributed to creating a coalition of women from two groups: organizations with a socialist affiliation of middle-class and professional women and groups of women from popular sectors ("pobladoras"). While central in delegitimizing the regime and mobilizing support for the democratic transition, the linkages and coalitions formed among women's groups faded once the transition took place. "In the 1990s, political parties took center stage and displaced social movements, including women's organizations" (Fernández Anderson 2021: 104).

With the return of democracy, Chile experienced another "feminist silence" (Kirkwood 1983).[28] Chilean women built a large and powerful coalition across

---

[27] "Queremos democracia en el país, y en la casa" (Adriana Santa Cruz, 1985). Quoted in Noonan (1995: 81).

[28] The concept of "feminist silence" comes from sociologist Julieta Kirkwood (1936–85) considered one of the founders of the Chilean feminist movement in the 1980s and gender studies in the country.

several organizations to fight for the right to vote. Once they conquered the right to vote, this effective coalition disappeared into thin air (Noonan 1995). Women's movements reorganized when a new generation of high school students, who had not experienced authoritarianism, began organizing to demand education reform, and eventually more sweeping social, economic, and political changes. Like in Argentina, Chile would experience its revolution of the daughters years later, culminating with massive mobilizations in support of women's rights and the first Constitutional Convention with gender parity.

3.1.2 Transition to Democracy and Feminist Silence on Abortion

Since the transition to democracy that began in 1990, legislators from the parties belonging to the Concertación presented a series of bills that sought to reestablish therapeutic abortions like what existed before Pinochet's dictatorship. The projects, nevertheless, were unsuccessful due to the opposition from parties within the same coalition that had close ties to the Catholic Church.[29] The opposition argued that the therapeutic label was confusing and it had the potential of leading to free abortions. Politicians' lack of interest in pushing for a divisive issue was accepted by most women who supported the Concertación, as Chile's newly re-established democracy found its legs (Baldez 2002).

At the beginning of the transition, women's organizations thought abortion was too controversial and decided to focus on areas where they could build consensus. The movement was also divided about the strategy to pursue abortion reform. Some in the movement thought they should demand to reinstitute therapeutic abortions, while others sought to pursue a more radical path toward complete legalization (Fernández Anderson 2021). After the transition to democracy, the left in Chile came to view feminism as a divisive and bourgeois issue. Their view would begin changing two decades after the transition with the student protests and the accompanying feminist movement. The lack of a strong and unified women's movement and a concerted push for reform left the complete ban on abortions unmodified until Michele Bachelet's second administration (2014–18).

In 2011, President Sebastián Piñera said that he would use his constitutional veto power if a therapeutic abortion bill was approved in Congress. In 2013, Piñera again expressed his rejection of abortion, stating that "the word abortion and the word therapeutic are essentially contradictory because abortion is an attempt against life and therapeutic is trying to save life."[30]

---

[29] The parties were the Christian Democratic Party (PDC), and the Alliance parties – the Independent Democratic Union (UDI) and the National Renovation (RN).

[30] This is part of President Piñera's speech during the presentation of the annual Human Rights Report on December 9, 2013. At that moment, Piñera spoke unequivocally in favor of life.

3.1.3 Michele Bachelet's Limited Achievement: Therapeutic Abortions

During her second administration, President Michelle Bachelet announced that she would promote a bill to decriminalize therapeutic abortions in cases of risk to the mother's life, rape, and viability of the fetus. The bill resulted from careful negotiations within Bachelet's electoral coalition to ensure it would pass in Congress (Fernández Anderson 2020). While "officials within the administration acknowledged the role of women's mobilization in including abortion in the government's program, particularly in light of its exclusion in Bachelet's first mandate" (Fernández Anderson 2020: 119), the bill itself never counted on the support of social actors such as women's movements, health care workers, doctors, lawyers, or unions. Ultimately, the bill was crafted in "a closed-door process" (120).

All groups – including members of her own government's coalition, civil society groups, and groups of women – were dissatisfied with Bachelet's exclusionary strategy. Moderate groups of women were dissatisfied with their lack of input in the legislation, and more radical groups of women were concerned reinstating therapeutic abortions was actually an attempt to block future discussions of full abortion legalization.

Bachelet presented the bill claiming that "the current regulations on the interruption of pregnancy, which prohibits it without exceptions, do not respond to the dignified treatment that the state of Chile must grant to its citizens. In this respect, our country is one of the four in the world that criminalizes abortion in all circumstances."[31] The government's exclusionary strategy to get the bill passed alienated allies who wanted a more inclusive debate that placed full legalization on the table, and intensified the discontent of those who opposed lifting abortion restrictions. In the end, Chile returned to the same abortion restrictions present before Pinochet's dictatorship without changing many hearts and minds, and without reaping any political reward.

3.1.4 Chile's Social Uprising and Feminism

The social unrest in Chile in 2019 highlighted the massive disconnect between the government and its citizens. The Chilean youth, especially high school and college students and feminist activists, had an active and visible role in the events that led to a new social pact and a planned rewriting of the constitution. Chilean feminist activists, especially those in their last years of high school and college, became politically active during the student protests that began in 2006.

---

[31] The countries were Chile, Nicaragua, El Salvador, and Malta. The message is from President Michelle Bachelet, Message No. 1230-362 on January 31, 2015.

The initial student mobilizations demanded changes in the curriculum, and later, in 2011, they expanded their claims to include free education.

The student movement was fearless and demanding. They were the first generation to be born after the end of the dictatorship and, as such, did not share the fear of government that their parents' and grandparents' generations had (Somma 2012). The students demanded a country without the legacy – institutional and cultural – of the dictatorship and adopted the provocative slogan, "Erasing your legacy will be our legacy" (Piscopo and Siavelis 2021).

Students were key actors in leading the protests that would escalate to a complete social crisis, the most important since the return to democracy. Responding to increases in Metro fares, students called for a mass refusal ("evade") to pay the elevated fees, which led to a series of actions that challenged the stability of Piñera's government. The call for evasion went viral on social networks, and in a couple of days, several stations and subway lines suffered interruptions due to the number of people avoiding paying for the service. In less than a week the number of evasion actions was so large that the Metro stopped providing services, leaving passengers stranded. As a result of the conflict at the Metro stations, fires, looting, and general protests erupted in the streets of Santiago (and beyond), and the president declared a state of emergency in the capital, allowing the armed forces to patrol the city alongside the Carabineros (Chilean's national police force). The President's declaration of a state of emergency failed to stop protestors and clashes with police. Army units, together with Carabineros, brutally attacked protestors, including firing ammunition and targeting protestors' eyesight.

On October 25, 2019, over one million Chileans marched in Santiago against inequality and a perceived lack of government responsiveness. In November, Congress agreed to hold a referendum on rewriting the constitution. By the time of the social uprising in 2019, many female activists had been participating in different political activities within the feminist movement of their high schools and universities for years. In several conversations with groups of four or five activists, many of them told us that it was the actions in the universities against sexual harassment, and the mishandling of the situations by faculty and authorities that pushed them to act politically. Many of those we interviewed were activists in the Communist Party and self-defined feminists, illustrating the depth of change in the party's incorporation of gender as an issue considerably different from class.

One young Chilean female activist described the social uprising of Chile as a "protest of emotion. Many people were crying, and there was so much trust among people who did not know each other; there was solidarity and a sense of fraternity."[32] These moments of emotion that several participants shared while fighting against the army and the police in the streets of Santiago were the same emotions activists would eventually share in the mobilizations for abortion legalization.[33]

Feminist movements are at the center of political, economic, social, and cultural changes in Latin America. A month after social unrest took over the streets of Chile, a feminist collective known as "Las Tesis" created a performance that became a national and international sensation, being repeated and performed in several countries in the region and beyond. "Las Tesis" defined their collective performance as an intervention to call attention to the inaction and complicity of the state, the president, the police, and the judges in girls' and women's rapes and femicides. It was first done in Valparaíso, Chile, where Las Tesis installed themselves in front of the Carabineros' police station in November 2019. Five days later, the video of the performance went viral after 2,000 Chilean women carried out the performance in Santiago.[34]

The intervention was translated into several languages and performed across the globe. Thousands of women performed the piece at the Zócalo, Mexico City's central plaza,[35] in Argentina, Colombia, France, Spain, and the United States. A group of feminist geographers (GeoChicas) documented that the intervention had taken place in over 400 locations in fifty countries (Figure 9).[36] When the intervention took place in Istanbul, Turkey, the police intervened by detaining several participants, leading female Turkish members of Parliament to conduct the performance in Parliament.

In the recorded videos of the interventions in Latin America, we observe the influence of NUM, as many women donned green handkerchiefs with classic NUM slogans. Testimonies collected from those who chose to participate in the intervention were unsurprisingly similar. Most of them stated that they were there for those who were no longer alive to have their voices heard ("por las que no están"), which was at the core of the NUM movement. The two other repetitive comments were about the "insanity" of the demand "to be able to be safe, to exist" as something that women should have to ask from the police,

---

[32] Author interview, April 2022.

[33] Many of the testimonies collected by the authors resemble the "emotion work" Deborah Gould (2006) describes in studying ACT UP activists in Chicago. Like in her work, emotions in this case seem to contribute to social movements' development and growth.

[34] www.youtube.com/watch?v=aB7r6hdo3W4. The intervention was one of the actions during the International Day to Eliminate Violence against Women (November 25, 2019).

[35] www.youtube.com/watch?v=gpAZbgOK6Ck.

[36] GeoChicas is a group of women who do mapping in OpenStreetMap and work to close the gender gap in the OpenStreetMap community. Geochicas have members in many continents. https://umap.openstreetmap.fr/es/map/un-violador-en-tu-camino-20192021-actualizado-al-2_394247#3/24.77/-25.93.

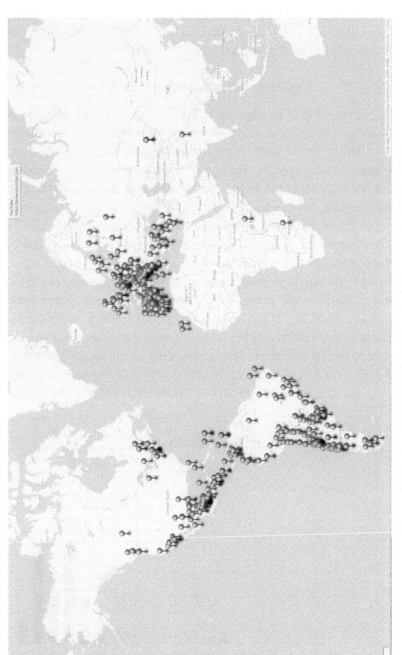

Figure 9 Mapping the "A Rapist in Your Path" intervention by Las Tesis
Source: GeoChicas

judges, and the state. Lastly, many women highlighted the massive size of the interventions and the sense of feminist solidarity across a growing social movement community. Being there with others who are strangers that share the same plight. Many of these interventions featured the common refrain that "Latin America will be all feminists."

3.1.5 Feminism and Abortion in Chile

Walking on the streets of Santiago, one can see the remnants of the graffiti from Chile's social uprising, and among them, murals dedicated exclusively to feminists' demands for gender parity in the constitutional convention, ending femicides, and legalizing abortion. Throughout Santiago, one can see the lasting strength and visibility of the feminist movement and its demands. Creating an inclusive feminist movement with young activists led to the first Constitutional Convention in the world with gender parity. It has also led to including an article in the constitution that, if approved, would provide abortion rights a constitutional status and protection. Surveys have revealed growing support for abortion rights. According to an Ipsos study from September 2021, about 73 percent of citizens approve of abortion under at least some circumstances. Some 41 percent think that abortion should be free and available through public health services, while 32 percent believe that it should be performed only under certain circumstances.

Figure 10 reveals the extent to which abortion rights activism has increased in Chile during the past decade. We uncovered very little evidence of protest events surrounding the issue from 2000 to 2010 in either of Chile's two largest

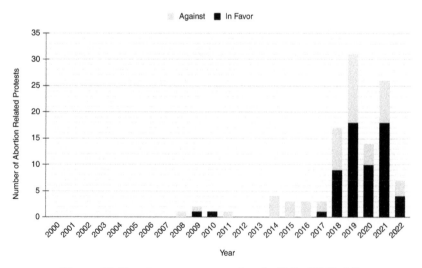

Figure 10 Abortion protests over time in Chile (2000–22)

newspapers. It is no coincidence that social movement activity surrounding abortion first appeared on the heels of student protests, and then surged amidst the arrival of NUM from across the Andes in 2015. Public opinion seems to have followed ramped up activism, as support for abortion increased from 64 percent in 2014 to 73 percent in 2021.

The constitutional proposal was unique because it is uncommon for constitutions to refer to abortion explicitly. Most constitutions refer to reproductive and sexual rights. Some scholars and journalists believe that including abortion in the constitution is an unwise political move. They argue that it alienates people who would have supported a new constitution but are antiabortion and, therefore, unlikely to vote for the constitution including a proabortion clause – indeed, the first version of the constitution was rejected by a plebiscite in September 2022. Feminist issues and demands are always seen as threatening and always asked to be put aside – particularly abortion, due to its divisive nature. We cannot predict what will happen in the future. However, we can draw some lessons from the feminist movement in the country.

3.1.6 Building a Feminist Collective in the Streets

In all our interviews with activists, the word "collective" came up repeatedly. All activists talked about their experiences in the movement as a collective struggle. Talking with other women about their experiences made them realize how much of their life experience was not individual but a collective experience of being a woman in Chile and Latin America. An example of this is the fear that many young women, most students, share in taking public transportation at night. A common experience among women is to ask each other to text – or send a message via WhatsApp – when they arrive at their destination so they know everything is ok. This informal system of check-ins enables women to feel protected, and the protection "insurance" for their well-being is in the hands of their friends. As it reads on the walls in Santiago "te protegen tus amigas, no la policía" (your friends protect you, not the police). Informal arrangements among women lead to building a collective identity. Feeling vulnerable and insecure being alone at night is not an individual experience but a collective and shared experience of women.

The framework is built on everyday experiences that had not been politicized before. Building on these collective experiences enables women to think and imagine their reality as a community. Moreover, as a collective, they fight together for abortion rights for all. The state should make you feel secure, but it does not. Even though you do not need or want to have an abortion, you should fight for those who would want and need to have one safely.

A sense of community was also present in the mobilizations. Testimonies from mobilizations in Buenos Aires, Bogota, Mexico City, and Santiago highlight the emotional intensity activists experienced on the streets and how those days changed them. Several of our interviewees in Buenos Aires and Santiago cried in remembering those days. Whereas several images of women on the streets showed them crying, the photos fail to capture the intensity of those feelings and how they have shaped the collective experience.

A word that came from the Argentinian streets was "sorority" ("sororidad") – the idea that women shared a common identity and purpose, a sisterhood that bound them with other women. This sisterhood also made them likely to demand justice for injustices done to others. In the case of abortion, it was a right for everyone based on the reality that those who were poor were the ones that were more likely to suffer the consequences of illegal abortions. Feminists in Chile told us that the abortion legalization movement in Argentina profoundly influenced them. Many of them told us that several of the chants ("cantitos") that they used in their mobilizations were borrowed from those used in the neighboring country: "We used the same songs. Why? Because they were good, we liked them, because we liked what happened in Argentina and wanted to happen here too. It was also a way to feel a connection with others, with feminists in Argentina that are like us."[37]

An activist remembered her experience of seeing images on the Internet and then living those images in her life:

> I remember seeing the images [of the mobilization] and dreaming that it would happen here [in Chile] and one day it happened [*sucedió*] . . . . Being on the streets with my friends and seeing in Santiago with my own eyes what I saw on the Internet in Buenos Aires was mind-blowing. Even telling it to you here, I get emotional. Reality . . . it's pretty unbelievable.[38]

3.2 Abortion Decriminalization in Mexico

Widespread feminist mobilization placed abortion on the agenda in Mexico, but the absence of a viable proabortion coalition in Congress meant that activists have had to pursue other avenues for advancing abortion rights. The case of Mexico thus illustrates the judicial path to abortion legalization.

In Mexico, abortion decriminalization was achieved through the Supreme Court and not Congress (see Figure 11 for a detailed timeline of the major events leading to abortion decriminalization). Immediately after Mexico City legalized abortion in 2007, twenty states changed their local constitutions to protect life

---

[37] Author interview, April 2022.   [38] Author interview, April 2022.

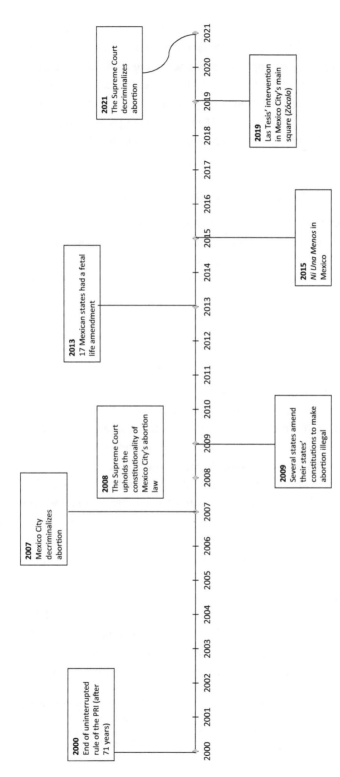

Figure 11 Timeline of the major events leading to the abortion decriminalization in Mexico

from conception.[39] Thus, the response to the capital's effort to expand reproductive rights was a considerable retrenchment of the same rights in other states. This patchwork of legislation implied that women living in Mexico had different rights and, therefore, different access to health care based on where they were living. The 2021 Supreme Court ruling put an end to this discrepancy by decriminalizing abortion in the country. The ruling also urges local and federal legislators to expand – not reduce – the conditions under which women can access abortion.

3.2.1 Abortion during One-Party Rule

Following the Mexican Revolution, the "Partido Revolucionario Institucional" (PRI) established the most durable one-party autocratic regime in Latin American history. Mexico is a federal system, and most states adopted criminal codes with similar language about abortion under PRI rule. All states banned abortions with exceptions reserved for cases of rape and to save the life of the mother. Just as the country began experiencing electoral competition in 1999, the case of Paulina gained national salience and spurred new discussion regarding abortion policy in Mexico.

Paulina was a thirteen-year-old from Mexicali, the capital of the state of Baja California, who was gang-raped during an armed robbery at her home. She became pregnant as a result of the rape and decided, with the support of her mother, to terminate the pregnancy. Despite the fact that all states legally enabled abortion in cases of rape, she was unable to exercise her right. The Catholic governor of the state of Baja California denied her access to legal abortion. Extensive media attention covered the case, leading to new discussions about abortion liberalization (Lamas and Bissell 2000; Cruz Tacarena 2004; Beer 2017).

In 2000, the uninterrupted rule of the PRI ended when, after seventy-one years of one-party rule, Mexicans elected Vicente Fox from the center-right "Partido Acción Nacional" (PAN). During the era of PRI dominance, the president and the national bureaucracy had complete control over policymaking at the federal and state levels. Subnational political actors were required to toe the party line if they hoped to rise through the PRI hierarchy. When the country abandoned one-party rule, state legislatures and bureaucracies regained autonomy to pursue considerable changes in public policy. Abortion, a moral policy issue, became an area

---

[39] Aguascalientes (2021), Nuevo León (2019), Sinaloa (2018), Veracruz (2017), Tamaulipas (2010), Chiapas (2010), Querétaro (2009), Oaxaca (2009), San Luis Potosí (2009), Yucatán (2009), Jalisco (2009), Nayarit (2009), Puebla (2009), Durango (2009), Guanajuato (2009), Quintana Roo (2009), Sonora (2009), Colima (2009), Baja California (2008), and Morelos (2008).

where there was stark variation across Mexican states. States where the Catholic Church was more powerful were more likely to ban abortions, whereas states where the "Partido de la Revolución Democrática" (PRD), a leftist party, was stronger were more likely to liberalize abortion restrictions.

3.2.2 Mexico City's Legalization and Backlash

In 2007, Mexico City decriminalized abortion during the first twelve weeks of pregnancy, and provided abortion access for free in public hospitals and government clinics. Feminist mobilization and the PRD control of the city's government explain this monumental step for reproductive rights expansion in the capital (Lamas 2009). Mexico City's decision to decriminalize abortion initiated a national debate about abortion policy, but instead of policy diffusion and adoption, the overwhelming trend was a backlash, as many states doubled down on abortion bans. When in 2008, the Supreme Court upheld the constitutionality of the City's abortion law, several states amended their states' constitutions to make abortion illegal, in some cases from the moment of conception, even in cases of rape and incest. Ultimately, the most notable consequence of Mexico City's push to legalize abortion was that "by the end of 2009, 15 states had adopted a fetal life amendment . . . [and] by 2013, 17 states had a fetal life amendment" (Beer 2017: 54).

The dramatic variation in abortion laws across the states meant that based on where they live, some women were able to get a legal and free abortion, while others could face prosecution for murder for having an abortion.[40] This inconsistency led feminist activists to pursue a judicial path to achieve consistency across Mexican states with regard to abortion decriminalization, in the absence of a viable strategy in the national legislature.

3.2.3 Abortion Legalization via the Judicial Path

Mexico is the country that birthed the concept and understanding of femicides as a result of the indiscriminate killing of women in Ciudad Juarez in the 1990s. The country's experience with femicide and the women's movements that made these killings visible had been working in the country consistently and uninterruptedly since Juarez with varying degrees of visibility.

The NUM movement was massive in Mexico, as evidenced by the throngs of women who attended the Las Tesis performance in the Zócalo. The growing visibility and strength of the feminist movement in the country has led to

---

[40] "In some of these states where a fetus is considered a person, women who have terminated pregnancies have been prosecuted for murder" (Beer 2017: 41).

significant changes in how politicians refer to violence against women, and similar to Argentina, paved the way for bridging claims from femicide to reproductive rights. On March 9, 2020, thousands of Mexican women participated in a general strike to draw attention to femicide rates in a country where more than ten women are murdered every day (Averbuch 2020).

Abortion rights organizations steadily gained more traction, inspired by the reproductive rights movement unfolding across the region (Figure 12). The initial uptick in activism occurred in 2018, following NUM and the initial legislative debate in Argentina. In September 2019, Oaxaca state legalized abortion in the first twelve weeks of pregnancy, providing wind in the sails of the growing national movement. Days later, abortion rights groups staged a massive mobilization in Mexico City that tens of thousands of activists attended.

The constant mobilization on the streets of the feminist movement was seen in full force as the Supreme Court of Justice considered the decriminalization of abortion in the country. Minutes after the Supreme Court's 2021 ruling became public decriminalizing abortion, feminist activists in the streets celebrated their victory. The hashtags commemorating the Supreme Court's decision became trends on Twitter – most of the hashtags (#QueSubaLaMarea) referred to the connection to the green wave feminist movements across Latin America. Most hashtags displayed green hearts symbolizing the color of the campaign for free and legal abortions, and activists displayed the green handkerchiefs during the street celebrations.

"Never again will a woman or a birthing person be prosecuted criminally. Today, the threat of imprisonment and the stigma that weighs on those who freely decide to interrupt their pregnancy are banished," stated the Minister of the Court, Luis María Aguilar, author of the opinion. His words echoed changes in public opinion observed in the country as a result of feminist activism and mobilizations. In 2005, only 12 percent of the country favored the legalization of abortion in all cases, according to a survey by the research firm "Parametria." A 2019 survey by the newspaper "El Financiero" found that nearly a third of Mexicans said they favor full legalization, and according to Ipsos more than half of Mexicans support abortion under certain circumstances, like danger to the life of the mother.

Politicians, regardless of their individual opinion about abortion, began changing their rhetoric to avoid taking polarizing positions on a controversial issue. For instance, asked about the issue hours before the Supreme Court's ruling, Mexican president, Andrés Manuel López Obrador, stated, "this is a question that women have to solve, the people have to solve it . . .. We have acted, in my case as President, with prudence and respect, because these are very controversial and polemic issues and we do not want to encourage any confrontation." López Obrador's response illustrates the new media strategy many politicians in the region are following. When in the past they expressed

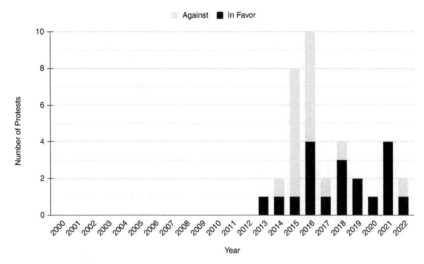

Figure 12 Abortion protests over time in Mexico (2000–22)

their opinions freely, they now risk angering a vocal abortion rights movement. In any case, feminist activists have not only changed policy but also the public and political discourse of the main actors in some of the countries with more clout in the region.

3.3 Trending toward Abortion Criminalization in Nicaragua

Not all Latin American countries are trending toward reproductive rights expansion. In 2000, the Nicaraguan National Assembly began discussing a new penal code to abolish therapeutic abortion (see Figure 13 for a detailed timeline of the major events leading to a total ban on abortions). The code counted on the support of the Catholic Church, Evangelical churches, and politicians from different parties (Heumann 2007). President Arnoldo Alemán led demonstrations aimed at banning abortion together with leaders of the Catholic Church in the country (Kampwirth 2003). Women's movements lobbied for a proposal that would extend access to therapeutic abortions. Discussions led to a postponement of the new penal code until 2003, when the case of Rosa led to renewed debate about abortion in the country.

3.3.1 The Case of Rosa

Rosa was eight when she was raped in a farming town in the central highlands of Costa Rica. She was there with her parents, who were working as sharecroppers. When Rosa began feeling tired and sick, her mother took her to see a doctor. After three days of observing what they believed to be a child with anemia, the

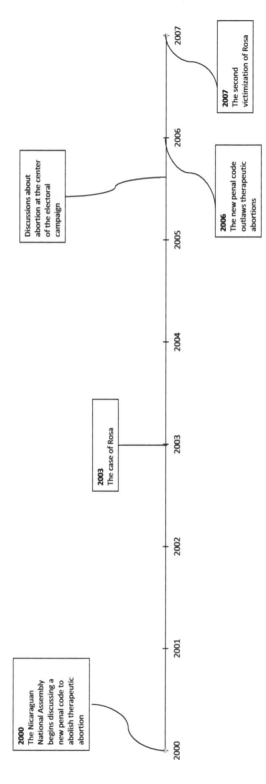

Figure 13 Timeline of the major events leading to a full ban on abortions in Nicaragua

doctors realized that Rosa was pregnant. Although abortion is legal in Costa Rica to protect a mother's health, social workers persuaded the family that Rosa should carry the child to term. Violeta Delgado, executive secretary of the Nicaraguan group that helped Rosa obtain the abortion, said that

> the Costa Rican doctors ... said get fruit, vitamins and baby clothes ... They did not give [the parents] information about the risks to their daughter. Nobody told them her bone structure wasn't developed, that her uterus was not the right size, and that she could have a spontaneous miscarriage and die. They treated her like any pregnant woman.

When news of Rosa's pregnancy became public through media coverage, Rosa's future and her pregnancy became embroiled in domestic and international politics. It took some time for the family to return to Nicaragua, where more turmoil awaited. Nicaragua's Health and Family Services ministers called on the family to force Rosa to give birth. The Catholic Church promised to provide care and housing for the infant. However, the family was worried that nine months of pregnancy would kill their only daughter. "We want this intervention to take place as soon as possible for her health and the well-being of our daughter," her father told television stations.[41] The family requested a medical consultation because Nicaraguan law required three doctors to certify that the mother's life was in danger before an abortion could proceed. Rosa and her family were kept in a safe house until the Attorney General ruled that the abortion was legal. A women's group took Rosa and her parents to a private clinic, where she took the pill that induced the abortion. There were no medical complications.

Rosa's case illustrated the power of antiabortion forces in Nicaragua. Powerful actors such as government ministers and the Church were willing to publicly go against the will of Rosa's parents, who were poor and illiterate "campesinos," to force their young daughter – the victim of rape – to give birth. The Minister of Family Affairs even called for Rosa to be taken away from her parents during the case, and the country's highest-ranking public health official declared that abortion was a crime. The Catholic Church noted that excommunication was automatic for anyone involved in the abortion – including Rosa and her family. By choosing to oppose Rosa's abortion publicly, the antiabortion movement successfully signaled their power and extreme opposition to reproductive rights expansion.

According to surveys carried out at the time, more than half of Nicaraguans (64 percent) thought that the nine-year-old should not be forced to carry

---

[41] The quote from Rosa's father comes from a report about the case published in the *Los Angeles Times* on March 23, 2003.

a pregnancy to term (Villegas 2003: 123). After the abortion, Rosa's parents relocated to Managua, the capital, fearful that they would be ostracized if they returned to their small community. Rosa, who was nine years old when a therapeutic abortion saved her life in 2003, was victimized again, and, at fourteen years old, she had a baby. In 2007, Rosa's mother reported to the Women's Police Station that her husband had abused her daughter for several years and was the child's father. The father recognized his paternity and left everyone wondering if Rosa's first pregnancy was also a result of his abuse. A Costa Rican citizen and neighbor of the family accused of raping Rosa was found not guilty, leaving a sense of impunity.

3.3.2 Sandinistas' Changing Views on Abortion Criminalization

Daniel Ortega, leader of the "Frente Sandinista de Liberación Nacional" (FSLN) returned to the presidency in 2006 after sixteen years out of power. His government was deemed part of a regional trend to the left defined as Latin America's "pink tide." At this time, there was a "real shift in the position of the Sandinista party, which had not legalized abortion when it was in power but had never before opposed therapeutic abortions" (Kampwirth 2008: 125). Ortega's views on abortion could be classified as ambivalent. Before his return to power, he opposed the practice due to its economic and political consequences, and not due to moral or religious convictions. Ortega envisioned abortion as an imperialistic tool for family planning to keep Nicaragua underpopulated and in a semicolonial state (Morgan 1990; Molyneux 2003). The antiabortion position he took in the 2006 presidential campaign contrasted with his previously held secular stance on most social issues (Kampwirth 2008).

Before the election, Ortega publicly reconciled with the Catholic Church. This reconciliation explains his surprising closeness with the influential bishop of Managua, Cardinal Obando. In the past, Cardinal Obando and Ortega had sparred on a number of issues (Lord 2009), and many saw this change of heart as a strategic move. The Sandinistas agreed to ban abortions in exchange for the support and votes of religious voters in a close race (Replogle 2007; Kane 2008).[42]

---

[42] "The FSLN new-found opposition to therapeutic abortion does not indicate an ideological shift to the right.[...] Rather than a shift to the right, it was a shift to cynicism. It was part and parcel for the FSLN's long-term evolution from a revolutionary party to one that was often a personal vehicle for Daniel Ortega and his family" (Kampwirth 2008: 127). "Seen from the perspective of Daniel Ortega and Rosario Murillo, it may be a left-wing project drained of principle or, to put it more kindly, a flexible left-wing project." ... "But whether flexible or cynical, the return to the left in Nicaragua does not look very left-wing, at least not from a feminist perspective" (Kampwirth 2008: 132).

3.3.3 Sandinistas and the Women's Movement

"The Nicaraguan women's movement had a long history of being openly critical of the FSLN" (Reuterswärd et al. 2011: 818). Whereas they supported the movement during the Contra War, they criticized its neglect of women's issues. By 1990, the divisions ran deep, leading women in the FSLN to declare themselves "autonomous" from the movement. The distance between the movement and the party widened further when the feminist movement supported Ortega's stepdaughter's accusation against him of sexual abuse since she was eleven years old (Kampwirth 2008).

While opposing Ortega, a powerful populist leader, the movement found itself divided about what was going to be the most effective strategy to decriminalize abortion. Some within the movement thought that demanding the right to therapeutic abortion was the most they could ask for, "the maximum demand, and don't even talk about legalizing abortion."[43] Others, in contrast, believed that the movement had been hurt by the moderation of their demands (Kampwirth 2008). The feminist movement's lack of unity in a strategy to fight for reproductive rights left them vulnerable against a stronger and united antiabortion movement.

3.3.4 Abortion and Ortega's Return to Power

In 2006, discussions about abortion were at the center of the electoral campaign. The Conservative Party (PCL), headed by the incumbent president Enrique Bolaños, sought to retain power in a tight election against the FSLN (Getgen 2008). Both parties supported a total ban on abortion. Whereas the most important women's movement in Nicaragua, the "Movimiento Autónomo de Mujeres" (MAM), succeeded in securing the support of the Minister of Health, the professional medical association, the United Nations, and several international NGOs, they did not succeed in blocking the proposal (Kampwirth 2008).

The Church is a key player in Nicaragua, with a sizable number of followers. Most career politicians were not eager to antagonize an important actor publicly by supporting a divisive and unpopular measure such as abortion. It also conducted mass-media campaigns, securing the support of the country's leading newspaper, "La Prensa," and staging a massive antiabortion rally in October 2006. Women's movements tried to lobby politicians and use the law to support their claims, but politicians refused to meet with or hear them, and the Supreme Court ignored their charges of unconstitutionality. "The Church's

---

[43] Interview with a feminist movement activist conducted by Kampwirth (2008: 128).

strategy largely succeeded and, in due course, won over twenty-five left-wing legislators who switched allegiance and withdrew their support for therapeutic abortion" (Getgen 2008).

With the 2006 election nearing, religious leaders pressured legislators to pass the bill before the election. Even with the opposition of the European Union and United Nations agencies, and others who requested to wait to vote on the bill until after the election, the National Assembly rendered a unanimous decision ten days before the election to ban all abortions (*El Nuevo Diario* 2006): "By repealing Article 165, the new penal code outlawed therapeutic abortions, which had been allowed under Nicaraguan law since 1870. A new penal code was approved, which made Nicaragua the sixth country in the world and the third in Central America to enforce a total ban on abortion" (Reuterswärd et al. 2011: 821).[44]

When surveyed following the passage of the ban, most interviewees did not seem to understand what a complete ban on abortions meant, and when asked about medical interventions to save the mother's life, they tended to disagree with the measure that the National Assembly had so hastily passed prior to the election.

> A poll conducted by CID-Gallup (2007) similarly found a large majority of Nicaraguans opposed to abortion (79 % against, 12 % in favor, 9% didn't know or didn't respond), but a significant percentage of those who opposed abortion favored it to save the life of the mother (55% in favor [44.45% of the total], 33% against, 12% didn't say or didn't answer). So, combined with the 12% who said they favored therapeutic abortion, 55.43% favored abortion to save the life of the woman (Kampwirth 2008: 130–32).

In our exploration of abortion-related protests covered in the two largest newspapers in Nicaragua, we found little evidence of proabortion mobilizations occurring during the past decade. As the country trends toward authoritarianism, and Ortega continues to crack down on opposition parties and even critical civil society organizations (Freedom House 2022), it seems that the women's movement might have missed any realistic opportunity to pressure the government to reinstitute therapeutic abortion in the foreseeable future.

4 Lessons from Latin America

In the preceding sections, we document the shifting tides in reproductive rights in Latin America, offer a case study of the successful mobilization for abortion rights in Argentina, and compare Chile, Mexico, and Nicaragua's diverging paths to rights expansion and retrenchment over the course of the past two

---

[44] See Viterna et al. (2018) for a detailed study of El Salvador.

decades.[45] In this concluding section, we also consider what we have learned, offering lessons from the aforementioned case studies. We focus in particular on what the abortion rights movement in the United States could learn from Latin America, in the wake of the Supreme Court ruling that overturned *Roe* v. *Wade*, which since 1973 has provided American women with the right to an abortion.

4.1 The Argentine Success Story

The case of Argentina highlights the importance of social movements in reproductive rights expansion. Abortion became law in Argentina due to a massive and inclusive feminist movement that was effective in mobilizing allies and persuading the general public. In particular, women on the streets pressuring the government to address gender violence and femicide placed abortion on the political agenda. In Section 2, we show how the massive and inclusive mobilization of NUM enabled women to construct a new social movement community that changed the country's social, political, and economic landscape. Women did not share a collective feminist identity before NUM, as feminism and feminist demands were relegated to academics and political activists. NUM made possible the creation of a massive and inclusive feminist movement.

Once NUM was created, a massive social movement community then transformed the claims to address gender violence into a campaign for abortion legalization. The case of Chiara Páez's family offers an illuminating example of this transformation. NUM began with the case of Chiara's murder, which served as a call to action in a country where violence against women had become quotidian. When women who had participated in NUM began mobilizing for abortion legalization, Chiara's mother opposed the movement. "Chiara was 14 years old, she was pregnant, and it was because of her that the NUM mobilizations began. I felt part of the first NUM, because it was not partisan, sectorial, religious, and because we all participated: women, men and children," said Verónica Camargo, Chiara's mother. However, as the movement began demanding abortion legalization, Camargo stopped participating. Nevertheless, Romina Páez, Chiara's sister and Camargo's daughter, strongly supported abortion legalization. She traveled from Rufino, Santa Fe, where Chiara was assassinated, to attend the historical Congressional voting session in Buenos Aires in 2018: "I have come to fight for the legalization of abortion because it is a public health issue. I think it is an essential right, no one can

---

[45] The Center for Reproductive Rights has an interactive map tracking the legal status of abortion in the region (and the world) in real time. They also had an infographic that illustrates changes in countries' abortion laws in the past twenty-five years. See: https://reproductiverights.org/maps/worlds-abortion-laws/.

force us to be mothers or make private decisions for us. It is a question of social justice."

The division between the Páez family – the mother and the sister of the victim who was the inspiration for NUM – is illustrative of the internal family dynamics we found while conducting research. They also highlight one of our key findings that has to do with the crucial role that the framing of abortion rights played in winning over allies. Unlike the rights-based language associated with the pro-choice movement in the United States, the Argentine movement made inroads by arguing that there is no banning abortion – if a woman wants one, she will get one. The only thing the state can control is how many women, particularly poor ones, die due to the unsafe nature of clandestine abortions.[46] This framing dates back to the campaign for contraception in the 1990s, but gained new reach when the women's movement harnessed the full organizational force of NUM.

The campaign's massive and inclusive character made it impossible to ignore women's demands. Feminists and feminist issues were given central space on television, and society began changing how they approach gender issues (Daby and Moseley 2022). President Alberto Fernández created a Ministry for Women, Gender and Diversity in charge of gender politics in the country, and the Ministry of Economy created a secretary ("Dirección Nacional") of economics, equality, and gender in charge of focusing on gender equality in the development of economic policies. Now that abortion is law, women activists have embarked on a new campaign to demand that the state recognize the unequal division of domestic work at homes in which women are in charge of care activities.

Finally, it would be impossible to end this Element without mentioning one of the key groups that propelled the movement: young women. The overflowing presence of young girls in every mobilization was unprecedented – young girls found in feminism their political identity. Interviewing dozens of them for this project, we found that many had not participated in politics before. Many did not identify with political parties and their platforms, but feminism moved them. "I don't believe very much in political parties, but I believe in feminism."[47] Feminism also enabled young women to connect with others and share their experiences, building a powerful sense of connection. And this collective was also inclusive. As we have documented, in the meetings to mobilize for abortion legalization, many young girls worked with others with whom they had little in common – in terms of class, place of residency, level of

---

[46] Infobae did a series of interviews with the Páez family. The family quotes come from a note written by Milton Del Moral (published on August 8, 2018).

[47] Author interview, April 2022.

education, and civil status. Yet they all shared the experience of discrimination and violence for being women. In the case of abortion, all of them share the experience of clandestineness.

In addressing what made her change her mind about abortion legalization, former president Christina Fernandez de Kirchner mentioned that she cared about how the future generations will remember her, particularly her grand-daughters. Many parents and grandparents who did not share their children and grandchildren's point of view about abortion began changing their positions when discussing with their children and listening to and reading about the subject. This change is reflected in public opinion polls that show how individuals have softened their antiabortion positions – particularly Argentine men. Mobilization made the difference. Only when hundreds of thousands of women took to the streets to make their voices heard, did the Argentine state and public start to listen.

4.2 Diverging Paths: Two Steps Forward, One Step Back in Chile, Mexico, and Nicaragua

The cases of Chile, Mexico, and Nicaragua illustrate different paths in expanding and retrenching reproductive rights. Chile's social uprising ("estallido social") changed the landscape of a country that had returned to democracy in the shadow of Pinochet, with a constitution imbued with the legacy of authoritarian rule. A conservative Catholic elite had always been successful in stalling social change. Chile was the last country in the region to legalize divorce, and it was late in legalizing same-sex marriage. Abortion, banned since the dictatorship, was only made legal under therapeutic conditions after Bachelet's careful negotiations behind closed doors within her coalition. While an advance, the manner in which the government achieved the reform, and the fact that abortion was only legalized under specific circumstances, was satisfying to few Chileans.

The social uprising of 2019 changed the set of political opportunities available to abortion activists, and more broadly, the place of the women's movement in the country. Women became central in the uprising, and a distinct feminist movement emerged within the government and in the convention that is set to write the country's new constitution. Without widespread student and women's mobilizations, abortion legalization never would have been on the table. Without the social uprising, Gabriel Boric, a former student leader and advocate for women's reproductive rights, would not have ascended to the presidency.

Chile's current government is largely composed of social movement leaders, and has signaled its plan to recognize women's rights, including abortion. In studying the women's movement in the country is important to highlight how it resembled, in its inclusivity, diversity, and youth, the women's social movement community in Argentina. In terms of the confluence of mass mobilization and a political environment ripe for constructing a winning proabortion coalition, Chile would appear to be the next Latin American country to join Argentina and Uruguay in the ranks of countries that have passed legislation making the right to abortion the law of the land. Chile might even go one step further, enshrining reproductive rights in the new constitution.

Mexico offers an alternative path to decriminalization. The Mexican case shows how federal countries are likely to present a patchwork of rules and regulations, ultimately leading to inconsistent outcomes based on geography. When Mexico City decriminalized abortion and provided it for free within its jurisdiction, activists thought that the ruling would expand the country's reproductive rights. Instead, several states responded by restricting access and penalizing women who sought out abortions, even under conditions that had previously been legal. In terms of reproductive rights, federalism implies considerable inconsistencies – this can disadvantage particularly poor women in more conservative, rural parts of countries, but it can also serve as the legal justification for more sweeping judicial interventions that seek to standardize reproductive rights access within countries. The Mexican case highlights the importance of the feminist strategy to rely on progressive courts in cases where conservative legislatures are unlikely to advance reproductive rights.

The apparent contrast we observe between Mexico and the United States is worth mentioning. As the Supreme Court in Mexico ruled to expand reproductive rights in the country, in the United States, the Supreme Court's decision to overturn Roe vs. Wade has significantly retrenched abortion rights, leading to the most significant transformation in reproductive rights in fifty years. With new restrictions on abortion access in a host of red states, including total bans, women in bordering states like Texas could potentially seek abortions in Mexico. We return to the United States below.

Finally, Nicaragua's backlash alerts us to the possibility of reproductive rights retrenchment. Our research consistently highlights the importance of an inclusive, diverse, and unified women's movement to advance the extension of reproductive rights. While Nicaraguan women had a long history of organization and political mobilization during the Sandinista revolution, the movement did not succeed in sustaining their strength and unity over time. Soon after the revolution, many women felt that the party did not address their demands and eventually distanced themselves from the party apparatus. In opposition, women could not build a social movement community to protect their reproductive rights, particularly as Nicaragua has descended further into a form of populist authoritarianism that revolves around Ortega. The union of the powerful Catholic Church with ambitious politicians overpowered a divided feminist movement. Seeing a political opportunity in a competitive electoral race, it was the Church that seized the opening to demand that candidates commit to criminalizing abortion. Desperate for the support of religious voters and undeterred by a relatively weak feminist movement, candidates conceded the Church their requested ban on abortion.

After supporting the Sandinistas and the FSLN against the Contras, the feminist movement found itself on the outside looking in. The rupture was total when Ortega's stepdaughter accused him of sexual abuse. While newly unified in rejecting Ortega, the movement failed to build a consistent strategy to stop the ban on abortions. Like feminists in Chile during Bachelet's government, feminists in Nicaragua disagreed about the best strategy to protect and expand reproductive rights. Whereas some thought the most effective strategy was to protect therapeutic abortions, others favored demanding full legalization. A divided movement was unable to mobilize support from conservative courts and politicians. It also failed in mobilizing people on the streets.

Feminists' disagreement on the proper strategy hamstrung the possibility of constructing an inclusive and massive movement. The lack of a coherent claim and mobilization frame has prevented the type of groundswell in support for reproductive rights in Nicaragua that we have observed across the region – in fact, we found very little evidence of major protest events in the past decade from our analysis of Nicaraguan newspapers. Conservative groups coalesced at the right time, led by the Church and allied with powerful politicians in an increasingly authoritarian regime. They showed how a unified strategy among conservative groups and alliances with ambitious politicians without a stated position on reproductive rights could be exploited to withdraw existing reproductive rights.

The cases of Chile, Mexico, and Nicaragua illustrate different paths to abortion legalization, decriminalization, and criminalization in the region. They show that activists could simultaneously pursue several paths to expand – or roll back – reproductive rights. The cases also highlight the key role of a unified and inclusive feminist movement. Without a consistent, resonant frame, the feminist movement will have a hard time organizing, mobilizing, and lobbying for its goals. Feminist movements are likely to succeed only in cases in which they successfully build a broad coalition to decriminalize abortion. In contrast to feminist movements, conservative groups have to this point needed only to protect the status quo. What those organizations do now that they are on the defensive, having lost on major legislative votes and court decisions, remains to be seen and merits further investigation.

4.3 The Conservative Backlash

Countermovements result from the success of progressive movements (Meyer and Staggenborg 1996: 150). The expansion of reproductive rights, and the legalization of abortion, provide conservative groups a target to advance their religious agenda. By making the personal political, feminist movements make "sexuality, family, and reproductive issues socially and politically salient" (Kretschmer and Meyer 2013: 405). Antifeminist movements also seek women's participation because their participation in these movements "is critically important in legitimizing a movement that seeks to control women" (Kretschmer and Meyer 2013: 394).

In Latin America, we observe how religious groups have formed interfaith alliances to band together to retrench reproductive rights. In contexts where these movements count on popular and grassroots support, progressive movements will likely have a more challenging time advancing their agenda. As massive and inclusive feminist movements spread across the region, we observe the response from interfaith alliances with strong grassroots support that "had the capacity to successfully organize massive social protests around moral agendas" (Gianella 2022: 139). As divorce and same-sex marriage became legal (and somewhat accepted) moral policy, abortion (and transgender) rights are the new targets for progressive and conservative mobilization.

Our research suggests that there could be high risks from advancing reproductive rights without supporting collective movements on the streets – in Mexico, for example, the effort to legalize abortion in Mexico City was led by the PRD, without an established and far-reaching grassroots movement within the rest of the country. The result was conservative groups using the Mexico City legislation to mobilize support for retrenchment in the states. Abortion legalization movements are likely to succeed when they count on the support of a massive and inclusive feminist movement on the streets, that can pressure elected officials and judges with mass mobilizations and at the ballot box.

The possibility of advancing progressive legislation in countries in the absence of massive activism does not seem promising. The cases of Argentina, Chile, Uruguay, Mexico, and Colombia show the importance of street activism in reaching a wider public, changing public opinion about abortion, and advancing sustained cultural changes. Decisions about abortion decriminalization and legalization in these countries counted on the sustained and massive support of feminists on the streets and relentless visible campaigns. When feminist movements in particular and civil society in general are disengaged from the construction of a legal strategy, progressive laws cannot trigger significant social changes. Examining strategic abortion litigation in Peru,

Gianella (2022) shows that the professionalization and specialization of Peruvian feminist NGOs allowed them to intervene effectively in the institutionalization of a gender perspective in official state politics. However, their lack of penetration and access to grassroots movements did not enable them to expand their successful legal mobilization while rendering precarious legal victories (Epp 1998; Gianella 2022).

The case of Peru offers a cautionary tale of the risks of legal mobilization decoupled from social movements. While the country counts on progressive feminists NGOs, their lack of autonomy given their international funding, hierarchical and nonparticipatory decision-making processes, and their deeply technocratic nature did not strengthen the feminist movement. Peruvian feminists are more connected to transnational networks of women in other countries than to women in their own country (that are not middle-class professionals). Consequently, the Peruvian feminist movement is weak as it lacks support from popular and grassroots organizations (Barrig 2002; Rousseau 2012; Gianella 2022).

There is a risk in imposing social change without the support of social movements on the ground. In the case of abortion, Peru offers evidence that professional and institutionalized feminist NGOs are unable to advance a progressive agenda on reproductive rights when they are unable to build an inclusive and massive feminist movement. Feminist NGOs that are exclusionary, due to their hierarchical and professional nature and lack of support from popular sectors, can impede success. The case is interesting because the 2016 NUM protest in Lima was one of the largest demonstrations in recent years. The mobilization brought media coverage to the topic, and encouraged a public discussion. It also led to the approval of new laws on gender violence and enforcement of existing laws to protect victims of gender violence (Rousseau et al. 2019).

However, the reaction to the movement was swift and massive with the creation of the movement #ConMisHijosNoTeMetas (Don't mess with my children). The movement was a reaction to proposed changes in the education curriculum to teach about gender equality ("enfoque de género"). Using the argument of gender ideology, the movement mobilized against an agenda they argued goes against the traditional family and favors homosexuality, abortion, transgender rights, and same-sex marriage.[48] Whereas the movement describes itself as nonpartisan and nonreligious, it has been identified with the Christian right, Christian fundamentalism, and Fujimorismo (named for populist authoritarian and former president, Alberto Fujimori, and his daughter Keiko). The

---

[48] Gender ideology is a new framing created to discard acceptance of anything different than binary sexual identification, heterosexual marriage, and family. This new ideology reframes the position of anti-gay, anti-trans, and anti-abortion groups in terms of rights to family, children, and religious people. "By stressing that a pro-LGBTQ agenda is an ideology or belief, they are

conservative actors that created the movement that started in Lima at the end of 2016, were effective in mobilizing an interfaith coalition of followers, leading to the resignations of two education ministers.

While the judicial path could provide victories on reproductive rights, these victories could be short-lived if they lack the support of an inclusive social movement community. Pursuing a legal strategy to advance reproductive rights also opens the door for a judicial backlash from conservative groups. "In striking contrast to progressive litigants, conservative actors, in alliance with religious groups who have deep grassroots movements and are well connected in Congress, have successfully responded to court outcomes by blocking bills to expand the grounds for legal abortion, and making abortion an important issue during political campaigns" (Gianella 2022: 113).

Progressive legislators are concerned about the counterproductive effects of the judicialization of abortion (Bergallo et al. 2018; Diniz and Carino 2019; Ruibal 2020). Whereas courts can be used to advance reproductive rights, when legal strategies are used without the support of inclusive and massive social movements the effect of judicial victories can be counterproductive. The judicial backlash can severely handicap legal strategies focused on advancing equality. One of the lessons of the Peruvian case is that progressive court victories could have limited effects and even unleash a solid conservative reaction when they do not count on civil society's support.

The growth of Evangelicals in Latin America has been accompanied by increased political clout and electoral influence. In Brazil, moral policy preferences increasingly guide candidate selection and voting behavior, which has deepened polarization and intolerance (Smith 2019). Studying tolerance for LGBTQ groups, Corrales (2021) finds more tolerance among the youth in all religious and nonreligious groups, except Evangelicals (Corrales and Sagarzazu 2019).

4.4 Lessons for the United States

On June 24, 2022, the United States Supreme Court overturned *Roe* v. *Wade*, enabling states to make their own decisions about abortion policy. In the following days, many women protesting the decision wore green handkerchiefs. A country in which abortion was a protected right for over fifty years now moves toward retrenching women's rights. Several politicians, actors, and celebrities made their rejection public. The decision came after three new

---

insinuating that it not a scientific proposition, and therefore, adults have the right to protect themselves and, more important, their children from exposure to it" (Corrales 2021: 40).

appointees by President Donald Trump, who in public hearings had publicly stated that Roe was precedent, voted to strike the ruling.

Our study of mobilization for abortion rights in Latin America shows how inequality in access leads activists to frame abortion as an issue of public health and social justice. As society was waking up to demand an end to femicide, activists argued that there could not be "ni una menos" as long as abortions were illegal. Women were dying due to clandestine abortions, and poor women were much likelier to die as a result of being unable to access clandestine health clinics, whereas middle- and upper-class women could abort safely. According to social movements' framing of the issue, abandoning illegality would save lives and make the country more just by protecting their most vulnerable citizens.

This difference in access should not be surprising to American readers who are now experiencing different abortion access based on their residence. Anticipating what would happen if Roe was overturned, the late Supreme Court Justice Ruth Bader Ginsburg explained that the effect would largely be restricted to poor women in anti-choice states. Many states would never outlaw abortion, and wealthier women will always be able to travel to those states, she pointed out:

> If you have the sophistication and the money, you're going to have someplace in the United States where your choice can be exercised in a safe manner. It would mean poor women have no choice. That doesn't make sense as a policy.[49]

The United States is headed toward a patchwork system like Mexico, where abortion access is determined by geography. Imagine two pregnant teenagers that decide they would like to have an abortion. One who lives in Portland, Oregon would be able to go to a clinic and have one; while the other who lives in Morgantown, West Virginia would not. Forcing a young woman to give birth and raise a child will have implications that will radically change their lives and hopes and dreams. It could also lead the teenager in West Virginia to pursue a clandestine abortion, putting her health and even her life at risk.

Our study focuses on the key role social movements play in abortion politics. We show that in cases where activists successfully built a massive, inclusive, and diverse feminist movement that supports abortion rights, abortion rights become obtainable. In contrast, when feminist movements are not massive, inclusive, and diverse, abortion rights is likely to be retrenched or not

---

[49] Interview with Justice Ruth Bader Ginsburg at the University of Chicago Law School in May 15, 2013: www.law.uchicago.edu/news/justice-ruth-bader-ginsburg-offers-critique-roe-v-wade-during-law-school-visit.

extended. Since the 1970s, the women's movement in the United States has become increasingly professionalized (Staggenborg 1988), and while certain organizations like NARAL have sought to build grassroots organizations in poor communities, the pro-choice movement in the United States is not as broad-based and inclusive as what we observed in Argentina, where slum-based organizations like "La Garganta Poderosa" were central in the legalization movement.

For example, similar to NUM, the recent #MeToo movement made waves in bringing attention to sexual assault and harassment, and even resulted in the arrests of prominent men in entertainment and politics. Yet unlike NUM it never became a broad-based movement to bring attention to women in the most precarious circumstances (Johnson and Renderos 2020), even as the movement was built on the community work of minority women (Luna 2020; Burke 2021). Likewise, the Women's March that occurred after Donald Trump took office drew hundreds of thousands of women to the streets, but nearly 80 percent of the women surveyed at the rally in Washington, DC were white, and 86 percent held at least bachelor's degrees (Fisher et al. 2017).

The evidence presented in this Element shows that the massive turnout of women on the streets has consequences. First, having thousands of women on the streets – who are all united by a common symbol, in the green handkerchief – makes it harder for society, politicians, and policymakers to ignore their demands. The visibility and strength in numbers were obvious to Argentine feminists, who chanted in their mobilizations: "Y ahora que estamos juntas, y ahora que si nos ven" (And now that we are together, and now that we are seen). Ignoring women's demands was impossible once those demands counted on the support of millions of bodies on the ground. Being silent was no longer an option.

Second, a massive, inclusive, and diverse feminist movement allowed women to gain space and visibility in mass and social media, giving them an opportunity to make their demands heard. Women and women's issues were given a prime position on television, radio, and social media for the first time. Conversations changed. Women and men's opinions about women's issues also began changing. The reckoning provided an opportunity for women to demand change, and they focused their demands on two issues: ending violence against women (NUM) and legalizing abortion. Importantly, these are two issues with which all women can identify, which facilitates the construction of a broad, cross-class and intergenerational social movement community.

Third, constructing a framework for abortion rights that accentuated the country's long history of human rights and social progress enabled activists to deploy a clear message and set of claims. In Argentina, social movements framed abortion access as intrinsically connected to social justice and public health. Rather than focusing on rights or "choice," feminist movements have argued that abortions happen whether they are legal or not. The only thing the state can do is ensure that they are safe. Since Argentina legalized abortion, activists in Mexico (2021) and Colombia (2022) have made similar arguments and joined the wave decriminalizing abortion.

The abortion rights movement in the United States needs a reset, and many abortion activists seem to realize it, as evidenced by a number of mobilizations in the aftermath of the *Dobbs* decision. For too long, abortion has been framed as an individual choice (a "rights" frame), which is antithetical to the construction of a collective movement and has allowed a strong countermovement to frame the issue in terms of "morality" (Rohlinger 2002). While we do not claim to be experts in American politics, we do reside in this country, and there seem to be four clear lessons from our research in Latin America for how women in the United States can turn the tide. One advantage that the US movement has is that the US population is already broadly supportive of abortion rights, which means the current objective is less about winning hearts and minds, and more about building political power in the streets.

The first lesson is the most obvious: women in the United States need to take to the streets with renewed vigor. Given the radicalization of the courts and the drift toward authoritarianism at the state level (Grumbach 2022), it seems unlikely that voting alone will allow women to reclaim reproductive rights. Some prominent leaders appear to recognize this. On the day that the Supreme Court officially overturned *Roe* v. *Wade*, New York Congresswoman Alexandria Ocasio-Cortez tweeted: "Voting is critical but alone it's not enough. We will need to organize, strike, fill coffers of abortion funds, open our homes to help those seeking safe passage, and more to establish and defend our rights. People have more power than they realize. It's time we rediscover it."[50] These mobilizations need to be sustained, and they must unapologetically connect abortion bans to violence against women – particularly poor women and women of color, who suffer the most under abortion bans.

Second, not only do abortion rights advocates need to flood the streets and exert pressure on elected politicians (particularly from the more sympathetic Democratic Party), they also need to do so with some kind of common symbol that bands them together. Our recommendation would be green handkerchiefs and attire, building on the success of abortion rights movements in Latin America. Just like pride flags have been important in building community among LGBTQ+ folks and their allies, green scarves and flags can serve as a unifying symbol

---

[50] Alexandria Ocasio-Cortez's Twitter account on June 24, 2022: https://twitter.com/AOC/status/1540478879881641988?s=20&t=RKgs7ZtiQiu2D0wXY-bUxw.

among people from diverse backgrounds that signals support for abortion rights in everyday life. Abortion prohibition affects everyone, whether they know it or not. Displays of support as everyday attire, on backpacks and purses, or on flags hanging from apartment windows and front porches would signal the strength of the movement and build a sense of solidarity among adherents.

Third, the way that abortion rights advocates in the United States frame abortion needs to change. The language of choice and individual rights was effective in the 1970s as a legal strategy, but as a call to collective action leaves much to be desired. "Choice" trivializes the importance of abortion access, and as abortion advocate Anat Shenker-Osorio argues, "makes women look careless. It feeds the opposition notion that women are using this as 'contraception.' And it cannot stand up to the rhetorical weight of life."[51] In their discussion of reproductive justice and the effort to move "beyond choice," Luna and Luker (2013) explain, "With the continued challenges to Roe, the symbol of the victory of the reproductive rights movement, many advocacy efforts centering on abortion and unwanted pregnancy continued to neglect the contributions of race and class inequality" (335). Treating abortion as an issue of individual liberty abdicates the state of any obligation to provide and protect abortion services, and atomizes women, treating abortion as something that happens to an individual, rather than a broader community of people. It also fails to reflect the experiences of the poor and women of color, who are disproportionately affected by illegality (Luna and Luker 2013).

Instead, abortion advocates need to make clear the extent to which banning abortion only bans *safe* abortion, with numerous devastating health and legal consequences for poor women and women of color in particular. In particular, focusing on the most restrictive state abortion policies, which in certain cases prohibit abortions even for women who have been raped, puts the antiabortion movement on the defensive. Certain antiabortion advocates have already run into widespread criticism for suggesting that pregnancy rarely results from rape.[52] Abortion saves women's lives. The abortion rights movement in the United States needs to frame it as such.[53]

In Latin America, individual cases where women have been victims of violence and injustice have served as sparks that have ignited movements. The case of Chiara Páez, similar to Breonna Taylor, Sandra Bland, and Black

---

[51] Interview in *Slate* Magazine on May 16, 2022: https://slate.com/news-and-politics/2022/05/abortion-activism-pro-choice-messaging-language-ireland-argentina.html.

[52] "GOP Candidates Downplay Possibility of Pregnancy from Rape": www.huffpost.com/entry/gop-candidates-pregnancy-rape_n_62ba6be0e4b06dcd46394591.

[53] Lawsuits along these lines have already begun in places like Texas, where uncertainties about what the circumstances are under which physicians can perform legal abortions have led women facing dire medical situations to leave the state: www.texastribune.org/2023/03/07/texas-abortion-lawsuit/.

Lives Matter, was so shocking and tragic that it motivated hundreds of thousands of Argentines to take to the streets and demand some kind of state response to gender violence. Unfortunately, similarly horrific cases are on the horizon in the United States in states where abortion is banned. Movement leaders need to leverage those cases to make the abstract personal, and build a social movement community that transcends class, age, and race.

Finally, abortion rights organizations need to attempt to cohere around one specific claim and throw their entire weight behind it. The most obvious goal would be to codify Roe as federal law. This has the added advantage of having been the status quo for fifty years, and builds on a widespread public disapproval of the Supreme Court's ruling overturning it. A fragmented movement that pursues different claims, with different targets, risks collapsing in similar fashion to what happened in Peru and Nicaragua. With a unified movement that speaks the same language and draws on common symbols of solidarity, reclaiming women's reproductive rights in the United States is possible. It is time for abortion advocates in the United States to look south as they chart a course forward.

Appendix

Qualitative Data

The qualitative data of this manuscript draws from a series of direct observations of feminist group meetings, in-depth interviews, recorded testimonies, and lengthy conversations that took place during and after the abortion debate in Argentina and Chile. In Argentina, we gathered evidence by attending meetings of social movements that participated in the campaign for abortion decriminalization in 2017, 2018, and 2019. We also interviewed female high school and college students from private and public schools and colleges. Our field diary notes from Argentina in 2018 and 2019 registered forty-seven conversations, fifteen with feminist scholars and journalists, and thirty-two with activists. We conducted follow-up fieldwork in April 2022 (during the COVID-19 pandemic) after abortion was legalized in Argentina. On our most recent trip, we had the opportunity to continue our conversation with community organizers, students, government officials, and university students. We have been conducting interviews with social movements for more than a decade, and discussions about abortion decriminalization have been ubiquitous in our fieldwork in the city and province of Buenos Aires and Mendoza province.

We visited Santiago on a research trip in April 2022 and conducted sixteen in-depth interviews with activists, students, scholars, and journalists. We spent much time walking the city with key informants and attending meetings to understand the depth, extent, and thoughts around the social change that was taking place in the country. We stayed in the Lastarria a couple of blocks from Baquedano, which was the epicenter of the social uprising. During our time, we interviewed government officials and close advisers to different groups of the Constitutional Convention which was taking place when we were there – we arrived a couple of weeks after the Convention has voted to include abortion rights in the draft of the new constitution. We had the opportunity to present earlier versions of this project to university students and received great feedback. As importantly, we were able to have frank and open conversations with young Chileans about their thoughts and lived experiences with the changes that were taking place in the country, especially about the emergence and strength of the feminist movement.

Beyond our field trips, direct observations and participation in local meetings, and in-depth interviews, we relied on the constant and comprehensive coverage of the movement in social and mainstream media. We followed more than 100 accounts on Twitter, Facebook, and Instagram, in addition to articles and testimonies from the selected countries' most prominent national newspapers.[1]

---

[1] We also consulted information gathered by Calvo and Aruguete (2020) for a forthcoming book about information, polarization, and conflict in social networks. In the book, the authors examine over four million tweets from the networks for and against abortion legalization during congressional discussions.

References

Alcántara, Manuel, and Cristina Rivas. 2018. "América Latina: Políticos más católicos, sociedades más plurales." Madrid: Estudios de Política Exterior.

Alcaraz, María Florencia. 2020. *¡Que Sea Ley!: La Lucha de Los Feminismos Por El Aborto Legal.* Vol. 67. Buenos Aires: Marea Editorial.

The AmericasBarometer by the LAPOP Lab. 2008–2021. www.vanderbilt.edu/lapop.

Anderson, Benedict. 1983. *Imagined Communities: Reflections on the Origin and Spread of Nationalism.* London.

Asociación Madres de Plaza de Mayo. 2020. *Madres de Plaza de Mayo: Nacimiento Del Pañuelo 7 de Octubre de 1977.* Buenos Aires: Asociación Madres de Plaza de Mayo. www.youtube.com/watch?v=0nx7ZylORto.

Auyero, Javier. 2003. *Contentious Lives: Two Argentine Women, Two Protests, and the Quest for Recognition.* Latin America Otherwise. Durham: Duke University Press.

Averbuch, Maya. 2020. "'We'll Disappear': Thousands of Mexican Women Strike to Protest Femicide." *The Guardian*, March 9,.

Baldez, Lisa. 2002. *Why Women Protest: Women's Movements in Chile.* Cambridge Studies in Comparative Politics. Cambridge: Cambridge University Press. https://doi.org/10.1017/CBO9780511756283.

Barrig, Maruja. 2002. "Persistencia de La Memoria; Feminismo y Estado En El Perú de Los 90." In *Sociedad Civil, Esfera Pública y Democratización En América Latina: Andes y Cono Sur.*, edited by Aldo Panfichi. Lima: Pontificia Universidad Católica del Perú, 213–246.

Beer, Caroline. 2017. "Making Abortion Laws in Mexico: Salience and Autonomy in the Policymaking Process." *Comparative Politics* 50 (1): 41–59. https://doi.org/10.5129/001041517821864408.

Benford, Robert D., and David A. Snow. 2000. "Framing Processes and Social Movements: An Overview and Assessment." *Annual Review of Sociology* 26 (1): 611–39. https://doi.org/10.1146/annurev.soc.26.1.611.

Bergallo, Paola, Isabel Cristina Jaramillo Sierra, and Juan Marco Vaggione. 2018. *El Aborto En América Latina: Estrategias Jurídicas Para Luchar Contra Su Legalización y Enfrentar Las Resistencias Conservadoras.* Buenos Aires: Siglo XXI.

Blofield, Merike. 2006. *The Politics of Moral Sin: Abortion and Divorce in Spain, Chile and Argentina.* 1st ed. New York: Routledge.

Blofield, Merike, and Christina Ewig. 2017. "The Left Turn and Abortion Politics in Latin America." *Social Politics: International Studies in Gender, State & Society* 24 (4): 481–510. https://doi.org/10.1093/sp/jxx018.

Boas, Taylor C. 2020. "The Electoral Representation of Evangelicals in Latin America." *Oxford Research Encyclopedia of Politics*. February 28. https://doi.org/10.1093/acrefore/9780190228637.013.1748.

Botero, Sandra, Daniel M. Brinks, and Ezequiel A. Gonzalez-Ocantos. 2022. *The Limits of Judicialization: From Progress to Backlash in Latin America*. New York: Cambridge University Press.

Boulding, Carew. 2014. *NGOs, Political Protest, and Civil Society*. New York: Cambridge University Press.

Brinks, Daniel, Steven Levitsky, and Maria Murillo. 2019. *Understanding Institutional Weakness: Power and Design in Latin American Institutions*. Elements in Politics and Society in Latin America. New York: Cambridge University Press. https://doi.org/10.1017/9781108772211.

Burke, Tarana. 2021. *Unbound: My History of Liberation and the Birth of the Me Too Movement*. New York: Flatiron Books.

Burstein, Paul. 2003. "The Impact of Public Opinion on Public Policy: A Review and an Agenda." *Political Research Quarterly* 56 (1): 29–40. https://doi.org/10.2307/3219881.

Buscaglia, Teresa Sofía. 2015. "#NiUnaMenos: Sin Banderías, Una Sola Consigna Será El Clamor de Todos." *La Nación*. June 3.

Calvo, Ernesto, and Natalia Aruguete. 2020. *Fake news, trolls y otros encantos: Cómo funcionan (para bien y para mal) las redes sociales*. Siglo XXI Editores.

Caminotti, Mariana. 2013. "La Representación Política de Mujeres En El Período Democrático." *Revista SAAP*, 329–7.

Casanova, Jose. 2007. "Rethinking Secularization: A Global Comparative Perspective". In Peter Beyer & Lori G. Beaman (eds.). *Religion, Globalization, and Culture*, 101–20. Brill.

Centenera, Mar. 2018. "Las jóvenes argentinas lideran en las calles la lucha a favor del aborto." *El País*. August 8. https://elpais.com/internacional/2018/08/08/argentina/1533757065_906612.html.

Clayton, Amanda. 2021. "How Do Electoral Gender Quotas Affect Policy?" *Annual Review of Political Science* 24 (1): 235–52. https://doi.org/10.1146/annurev-polisci-041719-102019.

Clayton, Amanda, Cecilia Josefsson, and Vibeke Wang. 2017. "Quotas and Women's Substantive Representation: Evidence from a Content Analysis of Ugandan Plenary Debates." *Politics & Gender* 13 (2): 276–304. https://doi.org/10.1017/S1743923X16000453.

Cohen, Mollie J., and Claire Q. Evans. 2018. "Latin American Views on Abortion in the Shadow of the Zika Epidemic." *LAPOP Topical Brief* 33.

Corrales, Javier. 2021. *The Politics of LGBTQ Rights Expansion in Latin America and the Caribbean*. New York: Cambridge University Press. https://doi.org/10.1017/9781108993609.

Corrales, Javier, and Mario Pecheny. 2010. "Six Reasons Why Argentina Legalized Gay Marriage First." *Americas Quarterly* (blog). July 30. https://americas quarterly.org/article/six-reasons-why-argentina-legalized-gay-marriage-first/.

Corrales, Javier, and Iñaki Sagarzazu. 2019. "Not All 'Sins' Are Rejected Equally: Resistance to LGBT Rights Across Religions in Colombia." *Politics and Religion Journal* 13 (2): 351–77. https://doi.org/10.54561/prj1302351c.

Cruz Tacarena, Rosario. 2004. "Análisis Del Discurso Sobre El Aborto En La Prensa Mexicana: El Caso Paulina." Centro de Investigaciones y Estudios Superiores en Antropología Social.

Daby, Mariela, and Mason W. Moseley. 2022. "Feminist Mobilization and the Abortion Debate in Latin America: Lessons from Argentina." *Politics & Gender* 18 (2): 359–93. https://doi.org/10.1017/S1743923X20000197.

Del Moral, Milton. 2018. "La mamá y la hermana de Chiara Páez, el femicidio que despertó el #NiUnaMenos, confrontadas por el aborto legal." *infobae*. August. www.infobae.com/sociedad/2018/08/08/la-mama-y-la-hermana-de-chiara-paez-el-femicidio-que-desperto-el-niunamenos-confrontadas-por-el-aborto-legal/.

Diani, Mario, and Donatella Della Porta. 2005. *Social Movements: An Introduction*. Oxford: Blackwell.

Dietrich, Bryce J., Matthew Hayes, and Diana Z. O'Brien. 2019. "Pitch Perfect: Vocal Pitch and the Emotional Intensity of Congressional Speech." *American Political Science Review* 113 (4): 941–62. https://doi.org/10.1017/S0003055419000467.

Díez, Jordi. 2015. *The Politics of Gay Marriage in Latin America: Argentina, Chile, and Mexico*. New York: Cambridge University Press.

Diniz, Debora and Giselle Carino. 2019. "É Injusto Acusar Movimentos Sociais de 'judicializar a Política'." *El Pais*. June 29.

El Universal. 2019. *"El Violador Eres Tú", Gritan En El Zócola*. Mexico City: El Universal. www.youtube.com/watch?v=gpAZbgOK6Ck.

Epp, Charles R. 1998. *The Rights Revolution: Lawyers, Activists, and Supreme Courts in Comparative Perspective*. University of Chicago Press.

Fernández Anderson, Cora. 2016. "Decriminalizing Abortion in Uruguay: Women's Movements, Secularism, and Political Allies." *Journal of Women, Politics & Policy* 38 (2): 221–46. https://doi.org/10.1080/1554477X.2016.1219583.

2020. *Fighting for Abortion Rights in Latin America: Social Movements, State Allies and Institutions.* 1st ed. New York: Routledge.

2021. "Abortion and Political Parties in the Southern Cone." Barbara Sutton and Nayla Luz Vacarezza 2021 Routledge Press, 29–49. *Abortion and Democracy: Contentious Body Politics in Argentina, Chile, and Uruguay.*

Fernández de Kirchner, Cristina. 2019. *Sinceramente.* Buenos Aires: Sudamericana (Penguin Random House).

Fernández Escudero, Clara. 2020. "'Ni Una Menos se convirtió en un nuevo Nunca Más': recuerdan la primera marcha contra la violencia machista." *Perfil.* June 3. www.perfil.com/noticias/sociedad/ni-una-menos-nuevo-nunca-mas-organizadoras-recuerdan-primera-marcha-contra-violencia-machista.phtml.

Ferree, Myra Marx. 2003. "Resonance and Radicalism: Feminist Framing in the Abortion Debates of the United States and Germany." *American Journal of Sociology* 109 (2): 304–44. https://doi.org/10.1086/378343.

Fisher, Dana, Dawn Dow, and Rashawn Ray. 2017. "Intersectionality Takes It to the Streets: Mobilizing Across Diverse Interests for the Women's March." *Science Advances* 3 (9): 1–8.

Franceschet, Susan, and Jennifer M. Piscopo. 2008. "Gender Quotas and Women's Substantive Representation: Lessons from Argentina." *Politics & Gender* 4 (3): 395–425. https://doi.org/10.1017/S1743923X08000342.

Friedman, Elisabeth Jay. 2009. "Gender, Sexuality and the Latin American Left: Testing the Transformation." *Third World Quarterly* 30 (2): 415–33.

Garay, Candelaria. 2016. *Social Policy Expansion in Latin America.* Cambridge: Cambridge University Press. https://doi.org/10.1017/9781316585405.

Gerring, John. 2004. "What Is a Case Study and What Is It Good For?" *The American Political Science Review* 98 (2): 341–54.

Getgen, Jocelyn E. 2008. "Reproductive Injustice: An Analysis of Nicaragua's Complete Abortion Ban." *Cornell International Law Journal* 41: 1. Article 8. 143–75.

Gianella, Camila. 2022. "When Winning in the Courts Is Not Enough: Abortion and the Limits of Legal Mobilization without Grassroots Involvement in Peru." In *The Limits of Judicialization: From Progress to Backlash in Latin America*, edited by Sandra Botero, Daniel M. Brinks, and Ezequiel A. Gonzalez-Ocantos, 112–46. Cambridge: Cambridge University Press.

Goffman, Erving. 1974. *Frame Analysis: An Essay on the Organization of Experience.* Cambridge, MA: Harvard University Press.

Gould, Deborah. 2006. "Life During Wartime: Emotions and the Development of Act Up." *Mobilization: An International Quarterly* 7 (2): 177–200. https://doi.org/10.17813/maiq.7.2.8u264427k88vl764.

Grumbach, Jacob. 2022. *Laboratories against democracy: How national parties transformed state politics*. Princeton University Press.

Halliday, Terence C., and Gregory Shaffer, eds. 2015. *Transnational Legal Orders*. Cambridge Studies in Law and Society. Cambridge: Cambridge University Press. https://doi.org/10.1017/CBO9781107707092.

Heagney, Meredith. 2013. "Justice Ruth Bader Ginsburg Offers Critique of Roe v. Wade During Law School Visit." *University of Chicago Law School*. May 15. www.law.uchicago.edu/news/justice-ruth-bader-ginsburg-offers-critique-roe-v-wade-during-law-school-visit.

Heumann, Silke G. 2007. "Abortion and Politics in Nicaragua: The Women's Movement in the Debate on the Abortion Law Reform 1999–2002." *Culture, Health & Sexuality* 9 (3): 217–31. https://doi.org/10.1080/13691050600859062.

Hochstetler, Kathryn, and Margaret E. Keck. 2007. *Greening Brazil*. Durham: Duke University Press. https://doi.org/10.2307/j.ctv1131c1g.

Htun, Mala. 2003. *Sex and the State: Abortion, Divorce, and the Family Under Latin American Dictatorships and Democracies*. Cambridge: Cambridge University Press.

Htun, Mala, and S. Laurel Weldon. 2018. *The Logics of Gender Justice: State Action on Women's Rights Around the World*. Cambridge Studies in Gender and Politics. Cambridge: Cambridge University Press. https://doi.org/10.1017/9781108277891.

Infobae. 2019. "Posturas opuestas sobre el aborto legal, la carta que jugaron Macri y Alberto Fernández en la recta final de la campaña." October 26. www.infobae.com/sociedad/2019/10/26/posturas-opuestas-sobre-el-aborto-legal-la-carta-que-jugaron-macri-y-alberto-fernandez-en-la-recta-final-de-la-campana/.

Johnson III, Richard Greggory, and Hugo Renderos. 2020. "Invisible populations and the# MeToo movement." *Public Administration Review* 80 (6): 1123–126.

Kampwirth, Karen. 2003. "Arnoldo Alemán Takes on the NGOs: Antifeminism and the New Populism in Nicaragua." *Latin American Politics and Society* 45 (2): 133–58. https://doi.org/10.2307/3176982.

Kampwirth, Karen. 2008. "Abortion, Antifeminism, and the Return of Daniel Ortega: In Nicaragua, Leftist Politics?" *Latin American Perspectives* 35 (6): 122–36.

Kane, Gillian. 2008. "Abortion Law Reform in Latin America: Lessons for Advocacy." *Gender & Development* 16 (2): 361–75. https://doi.org/10.1080/13552070802120558.

Kirkwood, Julieta. 1983. "Women and Politics in Chile." *International Social Science Journal* 35: 625–37.

Klibanoff, Eleanor. 2023. "Women Denied Abortions Sue Texas to Clarify Exceptions to Law." *Texas Tribune*. March 7. www.texastribune.org/ 2023/03/07/texas-abortion-lawsuit.

Kretschmer, Kelsy, and David S. Meyer. 2013. "Organizing around Gender Identities." In *The Oxford Handbook of Gender and Politics*, edited by Georgina Waylen, Karen Celis, Johanna Kantola, and S. Laurel Weldon, 1st ed., 390–410. New York: Oxford University Press. https://doi.org/ 10.1093/oxfordhb/9780199751457.013.0015.

Kubal, Mary Rose. 2012. "Transnational Policy Networks and Public Security Policy in Argentina and Chile." In *Comparative Public Policy in Latin America*, edited by Jordi Díez and Susan Franceschet, 176–204. Toronto: University of Toronto Press.

Kulczycki, Andrzej. 2011. "Abortion in Latin America: Changes in Practice, Growing Conflict, and Recent Policy Developments." *Studies in Family Planning* 42 (3): 199–220.

Lamas, Marta. 2009. "La Despenalización Del Aborto En México." *Nueva Sociedad* 220.

Lamas, Marta, and Sharon Bissell. 2000. "Abortion and Politics in Mexico: 'Context Is All'." *Reproductive Health Matters* 8 (16): 10–23. https://doi. org/10.1016/S0968-8080(00)90183-6.

Lapegna, Pablo. 2016. *Soybeans and Power: Genetically Modified Crops, Environmental Politics, and Social Movements in Argentina*. Global and Comparative Ethnography. New York: Oxford University Press. https:// doi.org/10.1093/acprof:oso/9780190215132.001.0001.

Loftus, Jeni. 2001. "America's Liberalization in Attitudes toward Homosexuality, 1973 to 1998." *American Sociological Review* 66 (5): 762–82.

Lopreite, Debora. 2012. "Travelling Ideas and Domestic Policy Change: The Transnational Politics of Reproductive Rights/Health in Argentina." *Global Social Policy* 12 (2): 109–28. https://doi.org/10.1177/1468018112 443685.

Lord, Sarah Helena. 2009. "The Nicaraguan Abortion Ban: Killing in Defense of Life." *North Carolina Law Review* 87: 537.

Luker, Kristin. 1985. *Abortion and the Politics of Motherhood*. University of California Press.

Luna, Zakiya. 2020. *Reproductive Rights as Human Rights: Women of Color and the Fight for Reproductive Justice*. New York University Press.

Luna, Zakiya, and Kristin Luker. 2013. "Reproductive Justice." *Annual Review of Law and Social Science* 9 (November): 327–52.

Machado, Fabiana, Carlos Scartascini, and Mariano Tommasi. 2011. "Political Institutions and Street Protests in Latin America." *The Journal of Conflict Resolution* 55 (3): 340–65.

Maffia, Diana, Peker, Luciana, Moreno, Alumine, and Morroni, Laura. 2011. *Mujeres Pariendo Historia. Cómo Se Gestó El Primer Encuentro Nacional de Mujeres*. Ciudad de Buenos Aires: Legislatura Porteña.

McAdam, Doug. 2017. "Social Movement Theory and the Prospects for Climate Change Activism in the United States." *Annual Review of Political Science* 20 (1): 189–208. https://doi.org/10.1146/annurev-polisci-052615-025801.

McCarthy, John D., and Mayer N. Zald. 1977. "Resource Mobilization and Social Movements: A Partial Theory." *American Journal of Sociology* 82 (6): 1212–41. https://doi.org/10.1086/226464.

Meyer, David S., and Debra C. Minkoff. 2004. "Conceptualizing Political Opportunity." *Social Forces* 82 (4): 1457–92.

Meyer, David S., and Suzanne Staggenborg. 1996. "Movements, Countermovements, and the Structure of Political Opportunity." *American Journal of Sociology* 101 (6): 1628–60. https://doi.org/10.1086/230869.

———. 2008. "Opposing Movement Strategies in U.S. Abortion Politics." In *Research in Social Movements, Conflicts and Change*, edited by Patrick G. Coy, 28:207–38. Emerald Publishing Limited Howard House, Wagon Lane, Bingley BD16 1WA, UK. https://doi.org/10.1016/S0163-786X(08)28007-9.

Molyneux, Maxine. 2003. "Mothers of Heroes and Martyrs: Gender Identity Politics in Nicaragua, 1979–1999 (Review)." *Hispanic American Historical Review* 83 (2): 419–21.

Morgan, Martha I. 1990. "Founding Mothers: Women's Voices and Stories in the 1987 Nicaraguan Constitution." *Boston University Law Review* 70: 1–107.

Moseley, Mason W. 2015. "Contentious Engagement: Understanding Protest Participation in Latin American Democracies." *Journal of Politics in Latin America* 7 (3): 3–48. https://doi.org/10.1177/1866802X1500700301.

———. 2018. *Protest State: The Rise of Everyday Contention in Latin America*. New York: Oxford University Press. https://doi.org/10.1093/oso/9780190694005.001.0001.

Noonan, Rita K. 1995. "Women against the State: Political Opportunities and Collective Action Frames in Chile's Transition to Democracy." *Sociological Forum* 10 (1): 81–111.

O'Donnell, Guillermo A., Philippe C. Schmitter, and Woodrow Wilson International Center for Scholars. Latin American Program. 1986. *Transitions from Authoritarian Rule: Tentative Conclusions about Uncertain Democracies*. Baltimore: Johns Hopkins University Press.

Osborn, Tracy, and Jeanette Morehouse Mendez. 2010. "Speaking as Women: Women and Floor Speeches in the Senate." *Journal of Women, Politics & Policy* 31 (1): 1–21. https://doi.org/10.1080/15544770903501384.

Otis, John. 2022. "Abortion laws in Colombia are now among the most liberal in the Americas." NPR. www.npr.org/sections/goatsandsoda/2022/05/10/1097570784/colombia-legalized-abortions-for-the-first-24-weeks-of-pregnancy-a-backlash-ensu.

Page, Benjamin I., and Robert Y. Shapiro. 1983. "Effects of Public Opinion on Policy." *The American Political Science Review* 77 (1): 175–90.

Pearson, Kathryn, and Logan Dancey. 2011. "Speaking for the Underrepresented in the House of Representatives: Voicing Women's Interests in a Partisan Era." *Politics & Gender* 7 (4): 493–519. https://doi.org/10.1017/S1743923X1100033X.

Pedriana, Nicholas. 2006. "From Protective to Equal Treatment: Legal Framing Processes and Transformation of the Women's Movement in the 1960s." *American Journal of Sociology* 111 (6): 1718–61. https://doi.org/10.1086/499911.

Pew Research Center's Religion & Public Life Project (blog). 2014. "Religion in Latin America." November 13. www.pewresearch.org/religion/2014/11/13/religion-in-latin-america/.

Piscopo, Jennifer M. 2011. "Rethinking Descriptive Representation: Rendering Women in Legislative Debates1." *Parliamentary Affairs* 64 (3): 448–72. https://doi.org/10.1093/pa/gsq061.

Piscopo, Jennifer M., and Peter M. Siavelis. 2021. "Chile's Constitutional Moment." *Current History* 120 (823): 43–49. https://doi.org/10.1525/curh.2021.120.823.43.

Pousadela, Inés M. 2016. "Social Mobilization and Political Representation: The Women's Movement's Struggle for Legal Abortion in Uruguay." *VOLUNTAS: International Journal of Voluntary and Nonprofit Organizations* 27 (1): 125–45. https://doi.org/10.1007/s11266-015-9558-2.

Przeworski, Adam. 1991. *Democracy and the Market*. New York: Cambridge University Press.

Replogle, Jill. 2007. "Nicaragua Tightens up Abortion Laws." *The Lancet* 369 (9555): 15–16.

Reuterswärd, Camilla, Pär Zetterberg, Suruchi Thapar-Björkert, and Maxine Molyneux. 2011. "Abortion Law Reforms in Colombia and Nicaragua: Issue Networks and Opportunity Contexts." *Development and Change* 42 (3): 805–31. https://doi.org/10.1111/j.1467-7660.2011.01714.x.

Roffo, Julieta. 2020. "Las diputadas 'sororas', el bloque transversal clave para que salga la ley." *elDiarioAR*. December 8. www.eldiarioar.com/sociedad/debate-sobre-el-aborto/aborto-diputadas-sororas_1_6488684.html.

Rohlinger, Deana A. "Framing the Abortion Debate: Organizational Resources, Media Strategies, and Movement-Countermovement Dynamics." *Sociological Quarterly* 43.4 (2002): 479–507.

Rohlinger, Deana A. 2015. *Abortion Politics, Mass Media, and Social Movements in America*. Cambridge: Cambridge University Press.

Rousseau, Stéphanie. 2012. *Mujeres y Ciudadanía: Las Paradojas Del Neopopulismo En El Perú de Los Noventa*. Lima: Instituto de Estudios Peruanos.

Rousseau, Stéphanie, Dargent, Eduardo, and Escudero, Aurora. 2019. "Rutas de Atención Estatal a Las Víctimas de Violencia de Género. Entre Legados e Innovaciones." Proyecto de investigación. Lima, Peru: CIES-PUCP.

Ruibal, Alba, and Cora Fernandez Anderson. 2020. "Legal Obstacles and Social Change: Strategies of the Abortion Rights Movement in Argentina." *Politics, Groups, and Identities* 8 (4): 698–713. https://doi.org/10.1080/21565503.2018.1541418.

Schwindt-Bayer, Leslie A. 2006. "Still Supermadres? Gender and the Policy Priorities of Latin American Legislators." *American Journal of Political Science* 50 (3): 570–85.

Shaw, Marcos. 2018. "La Cámara de Diputados Aprobó El Aborto Legal y Ahora Define El Senado – Infobae." *Infobae*. June 14. www.infobae.com/politica/2018/06/14/la-camara-de-diputados-aprobo-la-despenalizacion-del-aborto-y-ahora-define-el-senado/.

Singh, Susheela, Lisa Remez, Gilda Sedgh, Lorraine Kwok, and Tsuyoshi Onda. 2018. *Abortion Worldwide 2017: Uneven Progress and Unequal Access*. Washington, D.C.: Guttmacher Institute (pp. 1–64).

Smith, Amy Erica. 2019. *Religion and Brazilian Democracy: Mobilizing the People of God*. Cambridge: Cambridge University Press.

Snow, David. 2013. "Identity Dilemmas, Discursive Fields, Identity Work, and Mobilization: Clarifying the Identity–Movement Nexus." In *The Future of Social Movement Research: Dynamics, Mechanisms, and Processes*. 2013. Edited by Jacquelien van Stekelenburg, Conny Roggeband, Bert Klandermans. University of Minnesota. Minneapolis, MN.

Snow, David A., and Robert D. Benford. 1988. "Ideology, Frame Reference, and Participant Mobilization." *International Social Movement Research* 1: 197–217.

Somma, Nicolás. 2012. "The Chilean Student Movement of 2011–2012: Challenging the Marketization of Education." *Interface: A Journal for and about Social Movements* 4 (2): 296–309.

Somma, Nicolás M., Matías A. Bargsted, and Eduardo Valenzuela. 2017. "Mapping religious change in Latin America." *Latin American Politics and Society* 59 (1): 119–42.

Staggenborg, Suzanne. 1988. "The Consequences of Professionalization and Formalization in the ProChoice Movement." *American Sociological Review* 585–605.

———. 1994. *The Pro-choice Movement: Organization and Activism in the Abortion Conflict*. New York: Oxford University Press. https://books.google. pl/books?id=3oRBOuEvz30C.

———. 1998. "Social Movement Communities and Cycles of Protest: The Emergence and Maintenance of a Local Women's Movement." *Social Problems* 45 (2): 180–204. https://doi.org/10.2307/3097243.

Staggenborg, Suzanne, and Josée Lecomte. 2009. "Social Movement Campaigns: Mobilization and Outcomes in the Montreal Women's Movement Community." *Mobilization: An International Quarterly* 14 (2): 163–80. https://doi.org/10.17813/maiq.14.2.04l4240734477801.

Sutton, Barbara, and Elizabeth Borland. 2013. "Framing Abortion Rights in Argentina's Encuentros Nacionales de Mujeres." *Feminist Studies* 39 (1): 194–234.

Taladrid, Stephania. 2021. "Mexico's Historic Step Toward Legalizing Abortion." *The New Yorker*. October 28. www.newyorker.com/news/ news-desk/mexicos-historic-step-toward-legalizing-abortion.

Tarducci, Mónica. 2018. "Escenas claves de la lucha por el derecho al aborto en Argentina." *Salud Colectiva* 14 (3): 425. https://doi.org/10.18294/ sc.2018.2036.

Tarducci, Mónica, Catalina Trebisacce, and Karin Grammático. 2019. *Cuando El Feminismo Era Mala Palabra: Algunas Experiencias Del Feminismo Porteño*. Colección Desarrollo Social y Sociedad. Espacio Buenos Aires: Editorial. https://books.google.pl/books?id=45_dxgEACAAJ.

Tarrow, Sidney. 1994. *Power in Movement: Social Movements, Collective Action, and Mass Politics in the Modern State*. Cambridge: Cambridge University Press.

Tesis, Las. 2019. *Performance Colectivo Las Tesis "Un Violador En Tu Camino."* Santiago: Colectivo Registro Callejero. www.youtube.com/ watch?v=aB7r6hdo3W4.

Tilly, Charles. 2008. *Contentious Performances*. Cambridge: Cambridge University Press.

Turkewitz, Julie. 2022. "Colombia Decriminalizes Abortion, Bolstering Trend Across Region." *The New York Times*. February 22. www.nytimes.com/ 2022/02/22/world/americas/colombia-abortion.html.

Uranga, Mercedes. 2018. "Quienés son y qué dicen las referentes de las principales agrupaciones feministas" [Who are the leaders of the feminist movement, and what do they have to say]. La Nacíon, March 31. https://www.lanacion.com.ar/sociedad/quienes-son-y-que-dicen-las-referentes-de-las-principales-agrupaciones-feministas-de-hoynid2118535 (accessed May 5, 2020).

Villegas, Jairo. 2003. "Reaparece Rosa." *La Prensa*. March 16.

Viterna, Jocelyn, José Santos Guardado Bautista, Silvia Ivette Juarez Barrios, and Alba Evelyn Cortez. 2018. *Governance and the Reversal of Women's Rights*. New York: Oxford University Press. https://doi.org/10.1093/oso/9780198829591.003.0012.

Weeks, Ana Catalano. 2018. "Quotas and Party Priorities: Direct and Indirect Effects of Quota Laws." *Political Research Quarterly* 72 (4): 849–62. https://doi.org/10.1177/1065912918809493.

Weldon, S. Laurel. 2006. "Inclusion, Solidarity, and Social Movements: The Global Movement against Gender Violence." *Perspectives on Politics* 4 (1): 55–74. https://doi.org/10.1017/S1537592706060063.

Wood, Susan (Director), Lilián Abracinskas (Director), Sonia Correa (Director), and Mario Pecheny (Professor). 2016. "Reform of Abortion Law in Uruguay: Context, Process and Lessons Learned." *Reproductive Health Matters* 24 (48): 102–10.

Working Press. 2021. *Entrevista a Alicia Schejter // 36 Años de Lucha Por El Aborto Legal*. www.youtube.com/watch?v=Eyy4RkDWbxc.

Zald, Mayer N., and Roberta Ash. 1966. "Social Movement Organizations: Growth, Decay and Change." *Social Forces* 44 (3): 327–41. https://doi.org/10.2307/2575833.

Cambridge Elements ☰

Contentious Politics

David S. Meyer

University of California, Irvine

David S. Meyer is Professor of Sociology and Political Science at the University of California, Irvine. He has written extensively on social movements and public policy, mostly in the United States, and is a winner of the John D. McCarthy Award for Lifetime Achievement in the Scholarship of Social Movements and Collective Behavior.

Suzanne Staggenborg

University of Pittsburgh

Suzanne Staggenborg is Professor of Sociology at the University of Pittsburgh. She has studied organizational and political dynamics in a variety of social movements, including the women's movement and the environmental movement, and is a winner of the John D. McCarthy Award for Lifetime Achievement in the Scholarship of Social Movements and Collective Behavior.

About the series

Cambridge Elements series in Contentious Politics provides an important opportunity to bridge research and communication about the politics of protest across disciplines and between the academy and a broader public. Our focus is on political engagement, disruption, and collective action that extends beyond the boundaries of conventional institutional politics. Social movements, revolutionary campaigns, organized reform efforts, and more or less spontaneous uprisings are the important and interesting developments that animate contemporary politics; we welcome studies and analyses that promote better understanding and dialogue.

Cambridge Elements $^{\equiv}$

Contentious Politics

Elements in the Series

The Phantom at The Opera: Social Movements and Institutional Politics
Sidney Tarrow

The Street and the Ballot Box: Interactions Between Social Movements and Electoral Politics in Authoritarian Contexts
Lynette H. Ong

Contested Legitimacy in Ferguson: Nine Hours on Canfield Drive
Joshua Bloom

Contentious Politics in Emergency Critical Junctures
Donatella della Porta

Collective Resistance to Neoliberalism
Paul Almeida & Amalia Pérez Martín

Mobilizing for Abortion Rights in Latin America
Mariela Daby and Mason W. Moseley

A full series listing is available at: www.cambridge.org/ECTP